William Clark, Alexander Melville Clark

**Analytical summaries of the Patents, designs and trade marks' act**

1883

William Clark, Alexander Melville Clark

**Analytical summaries of the Patents, designs and trade marks' act**
*1883*

ISBN/EAN: 9783337108427

Printed in Europe, USA, Canada, Australia, Japan

Cover: Foto ©Suzi / pixelio.de

More available books at **www.hansebooks.com**

# ANALYTICAL

# SUMMARIES

### OF THE

# PATENTS, DESIGNS, AND TRADE MARKS' ACT, 1883,

### AND OF THE

# PATENT LAWS OF ALL FOREIGN COUNTRIES

### AND

# BRITISH COLONIES.

———

BY

## A. M. & Wm. CLARK,

### FELLOWS OF THE INSTITUTE OF PATENT AGENTS.

———

LONDON :

A. M. & Wm. CLARK, 53, CHANCERY LANE, W.C.

———

1884.

# PREFACE.

THE aim of the following pages is to furnish, in a form convenient for reference, a comprehensive analytical summary, not only of the new Patents, Designs, and Trade Marks' Act, but also of the patent laws of all foreign countries and colonies where patents or exclusive privileges are obtainable.

In the preparation of these summaries the object in view has been principally to supply information respecting such of the provisions of the various laws as affect the validity and duration of patents granted thereunder, as it cannot be doubted that the conditions which govern the obtainment and continuance of valid patents are of the highest importance both to patentees and purchasers of patents.

To the summaries of the foreign and colonial laws, some particulars of the manufacturing industries of the respective countries have been added, which, although necessarily brief, may be found useful to intending patentees.

BRITISH, FOREIGN, AND COLONIAL PATENT OFFICE,
53, *Chancery Lane, London.*

———

Applications for LETTERS PATENT, and for the
REGISTRATION of DESIGNS and TRADE MARKS, at
home and abroad, attended to.

SPECIFICATIONS drawn and revised ; opinions
given ; cases prepared for counsel, and all other
business relating to the Protection of Inventions
transacted.

————:O:————

MECHANICAL MOTION.—Plates of 125 Mechanical
Movements, with key, together with a Summary
of the new English Patent Law only, may be
had on application.

# GREAT BRITAIN AND IRELAND.

————:o:————

## PATENTS, DESIGNS, AND TRADE MARKS ACT, 1883.
### (46 *and* 47 *Vict., cap.* 57.)

## PATENTS FOR INVENTIONS.

### INTRODUCTION.

UNDER the new Act, which came into force on the 1st January, 1884, Letters Patent will be granted for new and useful Inventions at greatly reduced fees, and will confer the exclusive right to make, use, exercise, and vend the Inventions to which they relate, within the United Kingdom of Great Britain and Ireland and the Isle of Man (but not the Channel Islands) for the term of 14 years, subject only to the payment of the annual taxes hereafter mentioned.

By this Act the Laws relating to Patents for Inventions have been consolidated and amended, the whole of the previous enactments having been repealed with the exception of the Statute of Monopolies (21 James I., cap. 3).

The most important changes in the practice effected by the new Act are:—a reduction in the Government fees on application, and the substitution of annual taxes in lieu of the £50 and £100 duties heretofore payable; the extension of provisional protection from six to nine months; the postponement of the "opposition" stage until after the complete specification has been filed and is open to public inspection; and the creation of a body of

B

Examiners charged with the duties of generally supervising applications, with a view to ensure adequate descriptions, and due conformity between provisional and complete specifications, and of comparing applications relating to similar inventions which may be concurrently pending before the office, in order to avoid the granting of a patent for an invention contained in a previous unpublished application.

The effects of the principal changes made in the law are :—that the life of an English patent for a foreign invention will no longer be dependent on the duration of a previous foreign patent, as was formerly the case ; that a patent will have the like effect as against the Crown as it has against a subject ; that a patentee may be compelled to grant licenses under certain circumstances ; and that a patentee may be held liable in damages for unjustifiably threatening legal proceedings.

The reduction of fees is undoubtedly a move in the right direction, but it is an open question whether in the true interests of inventors themselves this reform has not been carried too far in respect of the fees on the application for, and granting of, the patent. This, however, is a point which experience of the working of the law alone can determine. The option of substituting annual taxes for the burdensome duties of £50 and £100 hitherto payable, is a concession as welcome as it was unexpected, and will prove a most substantial boon to inventors. This is a reform which we have long advocated, but scarcely hoped to see realized.

We cannot but regret that the term of the patent was not fixed at 17 years without possibility of extension (as in the United States of America), instead of the old term of 14 years being retained, with power vested in the Judicial Committee of the Privy Council of recommending an extension of the term in exceptional cases. This system has always appeared to us to work inequitably, both on account of the costly nature of the proceedings, and the extreme uncertainty of the results, and we have reason to think that had the duration been definitely limited to a longer period, without extension, the interests both of inventors and the public would have been better served, and an element of uncertainty would have been eliminated.

We think that the extension of the term of provisional protection from six to nine months is a mistake. Except in very rare cases the shorter term has been found ample to enable inventors to reduce their inventions to practice, and it is to be feared that the greater length of the term, coupled with the absence of any incentives to action in the shape of payments falling due, will induce such leisurely action on the part of inventors that but little more will be accomplished in the way of perfecting inventions before finally specifying than has hitherto been done in the shorter term available.

The postponement of the opposition stage until after the publication of the specification is to be regretted, inasmuch as oppositions on "open documents" must necessarily be much more expensive and will undoubtedly be much more frequent than under the system which has prevailed hitherto of opposing in the dark. The change in the practice does not seem to afford any advantages to inventors commensurate with the vastly increased expense it will entail on them and the difficulties which will be thereby thrown in their way, and although the new practice might to the uninitiated appear to be the most rational way of settling conflicting claims, those most conversant with patent matters are generally, if indeed they are not unanimously, of opinion that the balance of advantage is on the side of the old system.

In one respect the Act sets an example which might with advantage be followed in the legislation of almost every foreign country, namely, the omission of the highly objectionable clause of the old law, which made the duration of an English patent for a foreign invention previously patented abroad, dependent on the continuance of the previous foreign patent. This vexatious condition never did, and never could, effect any good object, and was at best merely a trap for the purchasers of English patents unaware of the existence of prior foreign patents, or unable to exercise any control over the duration of the rights of other persons, upon which, however, their own so intimately depended. That foreign governments (especially that of the United States) will follow so excellent an example by amending their laws in the same sense is a consummation most devoutly to be wished.

Inventors are to be congratulated on the omission from the Act of all power on the part of the Examiners or of the Comptroller, to determine what is, or is not, proper subject matter for the grant of Letters Patent, and to grant or refuse patents accordingly, except in very rare instances, where the use of the invention may be considered contrary to law or morality.

Patents will be granted at the applicant's risk, both as regards the subject matter and the novelty of the invention (so far as public knowledge extends), and this is undoubtedly the right course. The functions of the Examiners will be principally limited to a documentary examination with a view to secure, as far as is possible by any mere routine official examination, a proper compliance with the requirements of the law. It is, however, necessary in this connection to warn inventors that skilled assistance will be more than ever necessary in the preparation of the Specifications, not only to avoid delay and difficulty by prompt and efficient compliance with mere technical requirements, but if need be to defend their interests against adverse decisions arising from strained or unjust interpretations of the law, or from official misapprehension of the legitimate development of which inventions may be susceptible in their progress from first conception to practical realization. The alterations in the law do not affect the basis on which the validity of patents rests, and the notion, to which the system of documentary examination may lend color, that when a patent has passed the ordeal of an official examination its validity will be unquestionable, is entirely fallacious, as many confiding patentees will doubtless discover to their cost

Another word of warning may be permitted. . In view of the increase in the number of applications for patents under the operation of the new Law, and the no less certain increase in the number of *soi-disant* patent agents that will take place, it will be necessary for inventors to exercise more discrimination than ever in the choice of professional assistance, and it may not be out of place to here allude to the Institute of Patent Agents as comprising amongst its members those of the highest standing in the profession. Although it may not necessarily follow that every Fellow of the Institute possesses exceptional scientific knowledge and skill, yet the qualification of member-ship is some guarantee (to put it at the lowest), of his honesty and fidelity. This, although not everything, is an important con-sideration, having in view the glaring cases which have from time to time occurred of malversation by grossly incompetent persons professing to act as patent agents. To those familiar with patent matters, this warning may perhaps be superfluous, but to the inexperienced it may not be out of place. An inventor applying for a patent for the first time is generally surprised to find himself inundated with "touting" circulars. It is hardly necessary to say that members of the Institute of Patent Agents do not send out circulars of the kind referred to.

# ANALYTICAL SUMMARY

OF THE

## PATENTS, DESIGNS, AND TRADE MARKS ACT, 1883, WITH COMMENTS THEREON.

## PATENTS.

**Patents, to whom granted.**—A patent will be granted to the true and first inventor, whether a British subject or not, or to the inventor conjointly with any other person or persons, or body corporate. The words "true and first inventor" as here used must not be read in their literal sense, but as including not only the actual inventor himself, but also the importer of a new invention from abroad.

Previous to the Statute of Monopolies (21 James I. c. 3) the importer of a new invention was entitled at Common Law to a patent for the sole use of the invention, and the Courts have ever since construed the 6th Sec. of the Statute of Monopolies to mean the true and first inventor *within the realm*, and to include the mere importer of a new invention from abroad as well as the actual inventor. The general practice in the case of foreign inventions has consequently been to apply for patents in the names of agents here as communications from abroad, the recipient of such communication being regarded as the importer of the invention, and consequently in law the true and first inventor within the realm.

The new Patent Act does not alter the law in this respect, nor does it alter the practice except as to the form of the documents. Patents will still be granted to the first importer (including the recipient of a communication from abroad), who is in the eye of the law the first and true inventor. (See also under *International Arrangements* as to the rights of foreign inventors.)

Before applying for protection jointly with another person or persons, an inventor should be careful to have the intended rights of each of the parties properly defined by a written agreement, as it has been held that where a patent is granted jointly to two or more persons in the usual form each one may use the invention without the consent of the other, and without being liable to account to the other for any profits thereby made. *Mathers v. Green* (L. R. 1. ch. 29). A patent will also be granted to the legal representative of the inventor should the latter die without applying for a patent, provided the application be made within six months of the inventor's decease.

**Patents, for what granted.**—Every patent will be limited to one invention only (although more than one claim may be made), and may be granted for any new and useful invention being a manner of new manufacture within Section 6 of the Statute of Monopolies (21 James I. c. 3), including an alleged invention.

Inventions for which Letters Patent may be granted may be roughly classed as follows :—new or improved processes or methods (whether chemical or mechanical) of producing new or old commercial products, whether such processes or methods do or do not involve the use of special machinery or apparatus ; new machines, apparatus, or contrivances, for producing new effects, or for producing old effects in a more beneficial way, including new combinations of machinery or apparatus the constituent parts of which are old ; new modes of adapting a known thing to a new purpose provided that some inventive skill is displayed in such adaptation ; new articles of manufacture, including new commercial substances or compositions of matter whether produced by new or old means.

The Comptroller may however refuse to grant a patent for an invention the use of which would in his opinion be contrary to law or morality, but the applicant is entitled to be heard, personally or by his agent, in support of his application (§ 94), and probably to appeal to the law-officer.

**Novelty of Invention.**—The invention must be new within the realm, that is to say, within the United Kingdom of Great Britain and Ireland, and the Isle of Man. It must not, therefore, previous to making the application for Letters Patent, have been in use by the public, nor used in public by the patentee or any one else for commercial purposes, or otherwise than experimentally, nor manufactured and offered for sale; nor previously patented in the United Kingdom; nor so completely described that any person might have made it, used it, or put it in operation, in any printed book or publication published, circulating, or accessible to the public, in the United Kingdom. (See under *International Arrangements* as to the exception in respect of the publication and use in the United Kingdom of foreign inventions previously patented abroad.) A patent to the true and first Inventor will not, however, be invalidated by an application for Provisional Protection in fraud of him, or by any use or publication of the invention during the term of the Provisional Protection fraudulently obtained. The exhibition of an invention at an Industrial or International Exhibition, previous to the application for patent, will not invalidate the patent, provided certain formalities are complied with. (See *Exhibitions.*)

**Duration of Patent.**—The Patent is granted for the term of 14 years from its date, subject, however, to the payment of the annual taxes hereafter mentioned. (See *Taxes*). The duration of the patent is not dependent on any other condition, and is not in any way limited or affected by the duration of a previous foreign patent for the same invention, as in the case of foreign inventions under the previous law.

In exceptional cases the term of the patent may be prolonged. (See under *Prolongation.*)

**Date of Patent.**—The patent will date and run from the day on which the first application was made. (See *International Arrangements* as to the date of patents for foreign inventions.)

**Procedure.**—The application must contain a declaration by the inventor or importer (or, in the case of joint applicants, by one of the applicants), and must be accompanied either by a *provisional* or a *complete* specification, according as the invention is in an embryo or a mature condition.

A Provisional Specification must describe the nature of the invention with more or less precision, and must be accompanied by drawings if required. This document is kept secret until the Complete Specification is filed.

A Complete Specification must describe the invention, and the means of carrying it out in practice, in such a full, clear, and precise manner that any person possessed of ordinary skill in the art to which the invention relates would be able, by following the directions of the specification, to produce the same result without difficulty. The specification must be accompanied by drawings, if required, and must conclude with a distinct statement of what is claimed as the invention to be protected.

**Protection.**—In either case immediate protection is obtained. This protection is denominated "Provisional" or "Complete" as the case may be, and it enables the invention to be used and published by making and selling, or otherwise, before the patent is actually granted. Complete Protection confers the same privileges and rights as if a patent had been sealed on the date of the acceptance of the Complete Specification, except that actions for infringements cannot be commenced until the patent is actually sealed.

**Duration of Protection.**—The maximum duration of "Provisional Protection" is nine months, and of "Complete Protection" 15 months from the date of application, such term in either case forming a portion of the duration of the patent.

**Examination.**—Every application is referred to an examiner to report (*a*) whether the invention has been fairly described, and the documents are in due form, and (*b*) whether the specification comprises the same invention as that described in a previous application which is still before the Office. The examiner's report is not made public. In the case of an adverse report in the first respect, the Comptroller may, after hearing the applicant or his agent, require the documents to be amended.

The applicant may, however, appeal from the Comptroller's decision to the Law Officer, whose decision is final.

Notice of acceptance will be given by the Comptroller to the applicant, and until the application be so accepted the protection above mentioned does not accrue.

If the examiner reports that the invention appears to be the same as that described in a previous application then before the Office, the Comptroller will give notice thereof to both applicants, so that each may oppose the grant of a patent to the other if necessary, such opposition to be made at the opposition stage hereafter referred to. The Comptroller may, after hearing the second applicant or his agent (§ 94), determine whether the inventions are the same, and, if so, may refuse to seal a patent to the second applicant. The Comptroller's decision is subject to an appeal to the Law Officer, whose decision is final.

If a Provisional Specification be filed in the first instance, a Complete Specification must be filed within nine months from the date of application.

The Complete Specification will be referred to an examiner, to ascertain whether it has been duly prepared, and whether, upon comparison with the Provisional Specification, it describes substantially the same Invention. In case of an adverse report in either respect, the Comptroller may, after hearing the applicant or his agent, refuse to accept the Complete Specification until amended. The applicant may appeal from the Comptroller's decision to the Law Officer, whose judgment is final.

Inventors must bear in mind that, notwithstanding that a specification may have been accepted as sufficient by the examiner, its sufficiency may still be questioned in a Court of Law. The specification is, consequently, of the utmost importance;—it determines the validity of a patent, and does, or does not, give it commercial value. The specification is, in fact, the basis of patent property; its soundness is scrutinized as well for purchase as for piracy or evasion; a mistake in specifying a really valuable invention is often productive of endless litigation and loss.

Notice of acceptance will be given by the Comptroller to the applicant, and unless a complete specification be so accepted within 12 months from the date of application (except an appeal be pending), the application becomes void.

**Advertisement.**—The acceptance of the complete specification will be officially advertised, and the specification will then be open to public inspection.

**Opposition.**—Within two months after this advertisement, any person may oppose the patent, on the ground of fraud, or on the ground that the invention has been already patented in England, or that an examiner has reported that the specification appears to describe the same invention as that described in a previous application before the Office. In case of such opposition, the Comptroller will hear both sides, and decide on the case, subject to appeal to the Law Officer, whose decision is final.

**Sealing Patent.**—The patent will be sealed as soon as possible after the term for entering Oppositions has expired (or after judgment in the applicant's favor, in case of opposition), and not later than 15 months from the date of application, except in case of the death of the applicant; or of delay in consequence of an appeal to the Law Officer against the Comptroller's decision respecting the specification, or of opposition to the grant of the patent. In case the applicant dies during the above term, the patent may be granted to his legal representative, at any time within 12 months from his decease. Every patent will be dated as of the day of application (see exception in certain cases under *International Arrangements*), but proceedings cannot be taken in respect of infringements committed prior to the publication of the Complete Specification, and it will therefore be desirable to file that document without unnecessary delay.

In case of conflicting applications, the sealing of one patent will be no bar to the sealing of another on an earlier application.

**Extent of Patent.**—The exclusive privilege conferred by the patent extends to the United Kingdom of Great Britain and Ireland and the Isle of Man, but not to the Channel Islands.

**Taxes.**—After payment of the fees on application no further fees are payable on the patent for the first four years from its date, but its subsequent duration is dependent on the payment of an annual tax of £10 before the end of the fourth and each of the three subsequent years, rising to £15 before the end of each of the 8th and 9th years, and to £20 before the end of the 10th and each of the following years. Patentees have the option of paying up these fees in full by the payment of £50 before the end of the 4th year, and £100 before the end of the 8th year, but few are likely to avail themselves of this, inasmuch as the payment of £50 in a lump sum will only extend the patent for the same period as the payment of £40 in four annual instalments of £10 each. If by accident, mistake, or inadvertence, the tax is not paid in due time, three months' grace may, on proof thereof, be obtained for making payment, subject to a fine not exceeding £10.

The above mentioned annual taxes apply also to patents dated prior to January 1st, 1884, and upon which the £50 stamp duty has not yet become due or been paid. Therefore patents dated 1881 may be kept in force by annual payments commencing 1885, in lieu of the £50 stamp duty, which would otherwise have been payable in 1884. Similarly, patents dated 1882 and 1883 may be kept in force by annual payments commencing 1886 and 1887 respectively ; ~~but~~ patents dated 1877 and subsequent years, on which the £50 stamp duty has been paid, can ~~only~~ also be kept in force by the payment of annual fees in lieu of the £100 stamp duty in one sum before the expiration of the 7th year from the date of the patent ~~as heretofore.~~

~~The second schedule of the Act was at first officially interpreted~~
~~as entitling the holders of patents dated 1877, 1878, 1879, and~~

~~1889), to the option of substituting annual payments (amounting in the aggregate to £120), for the £100 stamp-duty in one sum, but it has subsequently been determined that the Act cannot be so read, and consequently those patents will not benefit by the Act.~~

**Amendments and Disclaimers.**—Amendments by way of disclaimer, correction, or explanation, may be made to the specification and drawings at any time, provided that the effect of the amendment is not to make the invention claimed substantially larger than, or substantially different from, that originally claimed. Such amendment, when made, will be deemed, for all purposes, to form part of the specification, but no damages can be recovered for infringements committed prior to the amendment, unless the patentee satisfies the Court that his original claim was framed in good faith and with reasonable skill and knowledge. The application to amend must set forth the nature of the proposed amendment, and the reasons for making it. The application and the nature of the amendment will be advertised, and may be opposed within one month from the date of advertisement. In case of opposition the Comptroller will hear the parties and decide the case, subject to appeal to the Law Officer, whose judgment is final In the absence of opposition, or if the opponent does not appear, the Comptroller will determine whether, and subject to what conditions, the amendment ought to be allowed. If leave to amend be refused, an appeal lies to the Law Officer, whose decision is final. All amendments must be registered. If an action be pending, amendments only by way of disclaimer, and not otherwise, may be made, and put in evidence in the action. The Comptroller is empowered, on request in writing, accompanied by the prescribed fee, to correct any clerical error in an application for a patent, or in the address of the registered proprietor.

**Conditions of Grant; working invention, importation of patented articles.** — The Act imposes no obligation on the patentee to bring his invention into practical operation in the United Kingdom in order to maintain the patent in force, as is the case in some foreign countries, and the importation by the patentee of articles made abroad in accordance with his patent is not prohibited. But the Board of Trade is empowered to compel the patentee to grant licenses under certain circumstances. (See *Compulsory Licenses.*)

**Marking patented articles.**—The law does not require patented articles to be marked as such, but it is usual and generally desirable to do so. Any person falsely representing an article as patented by selling the same with the word "Patent" applied thereto or by otherwise falsely representing that a patent has been obtained therefor, is liable to a fine not exceeding £5 for every offence.

**Compulsory Licenses.**—If the patentee refuses to grant licenses on reasonable terms, the Board of Trade may order him to grant licenses upon such terms as the Board may deem just upon the petition of any person interested and proof of either of the following facts :—(*a*) that in consequence of such refusal the invention is not being worked in the United Kingdom ; (*b*) that in consequence of such refusal the reasonable requirements of the public cannot be supplied ; (*c*) that in consequence of such refusal any one is prevented from working or using an invention of his own to the best advantage.

This clause is designed to prevent the manufacture of the patented invention being carried on exclusively abroad to the benefit of foreign manufacturers alone, to ensure the wants of the public being satisfied, and to prevent the owner of an improvement which cannot be used without infringing a previous patent (which might be for an impracticable invention) from being either wholly debarred from using his improvement until the previous patent has expired, or compelled to accede to exorbitant demands of the prior patentee.

Patents dated prior to January 1st, 1884, are not subject to the compulsory license clause.

**Prolongation of Patent.**—The original term of the patent may be extended by the Queen in Council for a further term not exceeding seven years (or in exceptional cases fourteen years) if, in the opinion of the Judicial Committee of the Privy Council, the patentee has not received adequate remuneration under his patent, regard being had to the nature and merits of the invention in relation to the public, to the profits made by the patentee as such, and to all the circumstances of the case.

The petition for extension must be presented at least six months before the expiration of the original term of the patent, and any person may oppose such extension. The extension of the term of a patent must be registered.

**Revocation of Patent.**—Every ground on which a patent might, before the Act, have been repealed by *scire facias* (which is now abolished), will be a ground of revocation. A petition for revocation may be presented by the Law Officer or by any person authorised by him. A petition for revocation may also be presented by any person alleging that the patent was obtained in fraud of his rights, or of the rights of any person through whom he claims, or by any person alleging that he or any person under or through whom he claims, was the true inventor of any invention included in the claim of the patentee; or of any person alleging that he or his predecessor in business had, before the date of the patent, publicly manufactured, used, or sold within the realm anything claimed under the patent. The revocation of a patent must be registered.

In case of revocation on the ground of fraud, a patent may be granted to the true inventor for the residue of the term of the revoked patent.

**Assignments.**—A patent may be assigned for any place in, or part of, the Kingdom, as effectually as if the patent were originally granted to extend to that part or place only. A patent is also transmissible by will, or by operation of law as in cases of intestacy or bankruptcy, and all assignments, transmissions, and licences must be registered.

**Existing Patents.**—~~These~~ *all existing* patents ~~only which are dated 1881, 1882, and 1883,~~ benefit by the option of substituting annual taxes, in lieu of £50 and £100 stamp duties (see *Taxes*), but they are not subject to the compulsory license clause, nor to the clause binding the Crown. (See *Crown*).

**Exhibitions.**—The right to obtain a patent, or its validity when granted, will not be prejudiced by the exhibition of the invention at a duly certified Industrial or International Exhibition, or by the publication of the invention during the Exhibition, or the use of the invention in the Exhibition (or its use elsewhere without the privity or consent of the inventor), provided that previous notice be given by the inventor to the Comptroller of his intention to exhibit the invention, and that a patent be applied for before or within six months from the opening of the Exhibition.

**International Arrangements.** — Power is reserved under the Act for making arrangements with the Governments of foreign States for the mutual protection of inventions. If such arrangement be made with any State, the applicant for a patent in any such State will be entitled to a patent in the United Kingdom in priority to other applicants, and the British Patent will be dated as of the date of protection in such State.

Application must be made, in the same way as for other patents, within seven months from the date of applying for protection in the said foreign State. The publication or use of the invention in the United Kingdom during that period, and prior to the application for the patent, will not invalidate the patent when granted, but damages cannot be recovered for infringements happening prior to the acceptance of the Complete Specification. Neglect to apply within the prescribed period does not, however, deprive the foreign inventor of his right to obtain a patent, but he loses his right of priority, and is placed on the same level as other applicants.

These provisions of the Act may also be applied to the British Colonies and India, but in no case do they come into force until specially declared applicable by an order of the Queen in Council.

C

**Crown**—A patent will henceforth have a like effect as against the Sovereign as it has against a subject, but the Officers of the Crown may use the invention on terms to be settled by the Treasury in case of disagreement.

**Legal Proceedings.**—Either the patentee or his assignee may maintain proceedings for infringement. The most speedy and effective remedy is by way of action in the Chancery Division of the High Court of Justice for an injunction to restrain the defendant from further infringement of the patent for an account of the profits made by such infringement, and for damages; and in all cases of importance an interim injunction should be applied for immediately after the issue of the writ.

Either the Court of first instance or the Court of Appeal may call in the aid of an assessor on the hearing of an action which is to be tried without a jury, unless the Court otherwise directs.

The plaintiff must with his statement of claim deliver particulars of the breaches complained of, and the defendant must with his statement of defence deliver particulars of the objections on which he relies ; such particulars of objections must, if the defendant disputes the validity of the patent, state the grounds upon which he disputes it and if one of those grounds is want of novelty, must state the time and place of the alleged previous publication or user. At the hearing no evidence will be admitted of any infringement or objection of which particulars are not so delivered.

Every ground upon which a patent might, at the commencement of the Act, be repealed by *scire facias*, will be available by way of defence to an action of infringement.

The Court may in such action certify that the validity of the patent came in question, and thereupon the plaintiff, if he succeed in any subsequent action, will be entitled to his full costs, charges, and expenses as between solicitor and client, unless the Court otherwise directs.

Any person who directly or indirectly uses a patentee's invention for the purposes of profit without his license is guilty of infringement. A mere colorable imitation of the invention, and which does not differ from it substantially, is an infringement. The substance, and not the form, of the invention is to be considered. The user in this country for the purposes of profit of an article manufactured abroad according to the specification is an infringement.

It has hitherto been too common a practice for a patentee, who is doubtful of the validity of his patent, to endeavour to intimidate others, and thereby to deter them from using the patented invention by threats of legal proceedings which there is no intention whatever to carry out. This practice, it is to be hoped, will receive a wholesome check by the present Act, which provides that where a person claiming to be a patentee threatens any other person with any legal proceedings or liability in respect of any alleged manufacture, use, sale, or purchase of the invention, any person aggrieved may bring an action against such patentee, and may obtain an injunction against a continuance of such threats, and recover damages if the alleged manufacture, use, sale, or purchase was not in fact an infringement of any legal rights of the person making such threats ; unless the person threatening, himself, with due diligence commences and prosecutes an action for infringement.

## DESIGNS.

The new Act repeals all previous enactments relating to the copyright of designs having for object some purpose of ornament or of utility, and consolidates and amends the laws relating to this subject, by providing anew for the registration of designs without making any distinction as to the character or purpose of the designs for which copyright is sought to be obtained.

The principal changes in the law of copyright in designs are :—(a) that the term of copyright and the cost of registration are invariable, whatever may be the character of the design or the nature of the material or article to which such design may be applied, the distinction as regards the term of copyright and the cost of registration which has hitherto been made between designs having some purpose of utility and designs of an ornamental character, and the distinction as regards the nature of the material, or of the article to which designs of the latter character may be applied, being thus abolished; (b) that the attribute of novelty, essential to the validity of the copyright, and which, under the repealed enactments, was required to be universal, is now required only in respect of the United Kingdom : (c) that the user of the registered design in the United Kingdom is, under certain circumstances, made obligatory ; (d) that power is taken to make arrangements in virtue whereof the proprietors of designs in foreign States and British Colonies may, under certain circumstances, become entitled to registration in priority to other applicants, and notwithstanding that such designs may have been published in the United Kingdom prior to the application for registration.

**Copyright, to whom granted.**— Copyright is granted to any person claiming to be the proprietor of any new and original design. (See also under *International Arrangements* as to the rights of applicants for protection of designs in foreign States.) The author of the design is deemed the proprietor, unless he executed the work on behalf of another person for a good or valuable consideration, in which case such other person is deemed the proprietor.

**Copyright, for what granted.**—Copyright is granted for any new and original design, whether it is applicable for the pattern, or for the shape, or configuration, or for the ornament of any article of manufacture (except sculpture) or for any two or more of such purposes, no matter by what means it may be applied. The Comptroller may, however, refuse to register a design of which the use would, in his opinion, be contrary to law or morality, but the applicant is entitled to be heard personally, or by his agent, in support of his application, and an appeal lies from the Comptroller's decision to the Board of Trade.

**Novelty of Design.**—The design must not have been previously published in the United Kingdom, but it may have been published elsewhere (see also under *International Arrangements* as to prior publication of designs forming the subject matter of applications for protection in foreign States). Publication by exhibition at an Industrial or International Exhibition, prior to registration, does not affect the Copyright, provided that previous notice be given, and the application to register be made within six months of the opening of the Exhibition.

**Duration of Copyright.**—The registered proprietor of a design will have copyright therein for five years from the date of registration (see under *International Arrangements* as to date of registration in the case of foreign designs), subject to the obligation to furnish exact representations or specimens of the design, either with the application or before delivery on sale of any articles to which the registered design has been applied, and to mark each article bearing a registered design with the prescribed mark, words, or figures denoting that the design is registered, and subject to the use of the design in the manufacture of goods in this country within six months of its registration if the design is so used in any foreign country.

**Procedure.**—The application for registration must state the nature of the design, and the class or classes of goods in which it is to be registered, and must be accompanied by a number of specimens, or of drawings, photographs or tracings of the design, sufficient in the opinion of the Comptroller to enable him to identify the design, whereupon a certificate of registration is issued.

The Comptroller may refuse to register a design (after hearing the applicant or his agent), but an appeal lies from his decision to the Board of Trade.

Registered designs are not open to public inspection during the existence of the copyright, but may be inspected by the proprietor thereof, or the bearer of his written authority, or a person authorised by the Comptroller or the Court, but in no case may copies of the design be made. After the expiration of the copyright, designs are open to public inspection and may be copied. On production of a design and its registration mark, or other means of identification, information as to the proprietor and as to the existence or otherwise of the copyright and the classes of goods to which it relates, and the date of registration, will be furnished. Designs are protected only in respect of the class or classes of goods for which they may be registered.

**Amendments.**—The Comptroller is empowered to correct any clerical error in, or in connection with, an application for registration.

**Fees.**—Such fees will be payable in respect of applications, registration, and other matters, as may be, from time to time, with the sanction of the Treasury, prescribed by the Board of Trade.

**Conditions of Copyright ; marking articles.**— Articles to which the registered design is applied must be marked with the prescribed mark, words, or figures, denoting that the design is registered, under the penalty of nullifying the copyright.

**User of Design abroad.**—If the registered design is used in manufacture in any foreign country, and is not so used within six months of its registration, in this country, the copyright will cease.

**Legal Proceedings. Penalty for piracy of Design.** —The unlawful application to any article, etc., of a registered design, or any fraudulent imitation thereof, in the classes of goods for which it is registered, for purposes of sale, or the publishing or exposing for sale of any article, etc., to which such design has knowingly been unlawfully applied, is punishable for every offence by the forfeiture of a sum not exceeding £50 to the proprietor, such sum being recoverable as a simple contract debt by action in any Court of competent jurisdiction. Or the proprietor may, if he prefers, bring an action for the recovery of damages.

**Falsely using the word " Registered."**—Any person selling articles with the word " Registered " falsely applied thereto or otherwise falsely representing a design as being registered, is liable to a fine not exceeding £5 for each offence.

**International Arrangements.**—Power is reserved in the Act for making arrangements with the Governments of foreign States for the mutual protection of designs. If such arrangement be made with any State the applicant for protection of a design in such State will be entitled to registration in priority of other applicants, and the registration in Great Britain will date from the date of protection in such foreign State. Application must be made in the same way as for other designs within four months from the application in such State during which period the design may be published, exhibited, and used in the United Kingdom without invalidating the copyright. Damages cannot however be recovered for infringements committed prior to the actual registration in this country. Neglect to apply for registration within the prescribed period does not however deprive the foreign proprietor of his right to obtain registration, but he loses the right of priority which he would otherwise have, and is placed on the same footing as other applicants.

These provisions of the Act may also be applied to the British Colonies and India, but in no case do they come into force until declared applicable by an order of the Queen in Council.

**Assignments, etc.**—The copyright in a design may be assigned or transmitted by will, or by operation of law as in cases of intestacy or bankruptcy. All notifications of Assignments, and of transmissions of registered designs, must be entered on the " Register of Designs."

## TRADE MARKS.

The new Act repeals the Trade Marks Acts of 1875, 1876 and 1877, and virtually re-enacts the same law with some modifications. The only important changes in the law are :— *(a)* that a fancy word not in common use may now be registered as a new mark ; *(b)* that the definition of a trade mark which may now be registered as an old mark is enlarged; *(c)* that registration of a trade mark now confers the exclusive right to use it in any other color which the owner may select at will, so that the penalty for infringement cannot in any case be evaded by changing the color whilst retaining the other characteristics of the mark ; *(d)* that the applicant may appeal from the decision of the Comptroller to the Board of Trade, instead of directly to the Court ; *(e)* that power is taken to make arrangements in virtue whereof the proprietors of trade marks in foreign States and British Colonies may, under certain circumstances become entitled to registration in priority of other applicants.

Under the new Act a trade mark may be registered on the application of the proprietor thereof in respect of particular goods or classes of goods. Registration of a trade mark is equivalent to public use of the mark, and is *primâ facie* evidence of the right of the registered proprietor thereof to the exclusive use of the mark, and after five years from the date of registration is conclusive evidence of such right subject to the provisions of the Act. A trade mark may be registered in any color, and such registration confers the exclusive right to use it in that or any other color.

No proceedings for infringement of a mark can be instituted until the mark has been registered, or in the case of an old mark—that is, a mark in use before 13th August, 1875—until registration has been refused.

Registration may be refused by the Comptroller after hearing the applicant ( § 94 ) subject to appeal to the Board of Trade, who may either decide the matter or refer the same to the High Court of Justice.

**Registration, to whom granted.**—Registration may be granted to any person, firm, or corporate body claiming to be the proprietor of the trade mark. (See also under *International Arrangements* as to the prior right of the owner of a foreign trade mark).

**Definition of a Trade Mark.**—The Law distinguishes between trade marks which have been used as such, prior to August 13th, 1875, and those adopted since that date.

The former are hereafter designated *old* marks and the latter *new* marks.

A *new* mark must consist of, or contain, at least one of the following essential particulars, viz. :—

(*a*) The name of an individual or firm printed, impressed, or woven, in some particular and distinctive manner ; or

(*b*) A written signature, or copy of a written signature, of the individual or firm applying for registration.

(*c*) A distinctive device, mark, brand, heading, label, ticket, or fancy word or words not in common use.

To any one or more of these essential particulars there may be added any letters, words, or figures, or combination thereof ; or any distinctive word or combination of words, even though the same is common to the trade, provided such common features be disclaimed.

But an *old* mark, consisting of any special and distinctive word or words, letter, figure, or combination of letters or figures, or of both, may be registered, and any distinctive device, mark, brand, heading, label, ticket, letter, word, or figure, or combination of letters, words, or figures, even though the same is common to the trade, may be added thereto, provided such common features be disclaimed, which disclaimer will be entered on the register.

In either case any such feature is deemed common to the

trade if it was publicly used by more than three persons on the same or similar goods before August 13th, 1875.

Any words, the exclusive use of which would not be deemed entitled to protection in a court of justice by reason of their deceptive character, or otherwise, or any scandalous design, may not be registered. The Comptroller may also refuse to register a trade mark, of which the use would in his opinion be contrary to law or morality, but the applicant is entitled to be heard personally or by his agent in support of his application ( § 94 ) and an appeal lies from the Comptroller's decision to the Board of Trade ( § 62 sub sec. 6 ). A number of trade marks indentical in their essential particulars, but varying only in statements of goods, prices, qualities, numbers, or names of places, may be registered as a series in one application.

**Duration of Right to Trade Mark.**—The duration of the right acquired by registration is unlimited, subject only to the payment of a small fee before the expiration of the first fourteen years, and each successive period of fourteen years from the date of registration. The right is, however, determinable with the goodwill of the business concerned in the goods for which it has been registered.

**Extent and Date of Right.**—The exclusive right conferred by registration extends to the United Kingdom of Great Britain and Ireland and the Isle of Man, and dates from the date of issue of the Certificate of Registration. (See also under *International Arrangements* as to date of registration in the case of foreign trade marks.)

**Procedure.**—An application must be accompanied by the prescribed number of drawings or specimens of the trade mark, and must state the particular goods to which it is to be applied. If no similar mark be already on the register, in respect of the same description of goods, the application will be advertised, and opposition to the registration may be entered within two months from such advertisement. Two months more are allowed to the applicant to reply to the opposition, whereupon the opponent will be called upon to give security for costs. The case will then be complete for hearing by the High Court of Justice. Should no opposition be entered registration of the mark will be proceeded with in due course. The application will be deemed abandoned if not completed within twelve months from the date of the application, owing to the applicant's default.

**Official Examination.**—Before any application for registration is passed by the Registrar, the register will be searched to ascertain whether the mark for which registration is sought so nearly resembles any other mark already on the register, in respect of the same description of goods, as to be calculated to deceive, in which case registration will be refused. Besides the marks actually on the register, those which have been on, but have been removed within the space of five years, also constitute a bar to the registration of a similar mark for similar goods.

**Renewal of Registration.**—The registration is subject to the payment of a small fee once every fourteen years, three months' grace being allowed, subject to a fine. Failing such payment the mark will be removed from the register. A discretionary power is vested in the Comptroller to restore to the register a mark so removed.

**Amendments.**—The Comptroller is empowered, upon application duly made, to correct clerical errors in the entry of a trade mark, or cancel any part of such entry, and the Court is empowered to grant leave to add to or alter a registered trade mark in any minor particular.

**International Arrangements respecting foreign Trade Marks.**—Power is reserved in the Act for making arrangements with the Governments of foreign States for the mutual protection of trade marks. If such arrangement be made with any State, the applicant for protection of a trade mark in such State will be entitled to registration in the United Kingdom in priority to other applicants, and the registration in Great Britain will date from the date of protec-

tion in such foreign State. Application must be made in
the same way as for other marks, and within four months
from the date of application in such State. Damages cannot,
however, be recovered for infringements committed prior to the
actual registration in this country. Neglect to apply within
the prescribed period does not, however, deprive the foreign
proprietor of all right to obtain registration, but he loses his
right of priority, and is placed on the same level as other
applicants. Any trade mark for which registration has been
duly applied in the country of origin, may be registered.

These provisions of the Act may also be applied to the British
Colonies and India, but in no case do they come into force until
specially declared applicable by an Order of the Queen in
Council.

**Falsely using word " Registered."** — Any person
falsely marking or representing a trade mark as " Registered,"
is liable to a fine not exceeding £5 for each offence.

**Assignment of Trade Mark**. — A registered trade
mark may be assigned or transmitted by will, or by operation
of law as in cases of intestacy or bankruptcy, and can only be
so assigned or transmitted in connection with the goodwill of
the business concerned in the goods for which it has been
registered. Notification of assignments, and of transmissions
of trade marks, must be entered in the "Register of Trade
Marks."

**Legal Proceedings**. — The registered proprietor of a
trade mark, that is to say, the person whose name appears on
the register, is entitled to the exclusive use thereof. The most
efficacious remedy in the case of an infringement is by way of
action against the offender in the Chancery Division of the
High Court of Justice for an injunction, an account, and
damages ; and the Court should be moved for an interim
injunction immediately after the issue of the writ.

No proceeding can be instituted for the infringement of a
trade mark unless the same has been registered, or, in the case

of a Trade Mark in use before the 13th of August, 1875, registration thereof has been refused.   The Comptroller may grant a certificate of refusal of registration.

## COST OF OBTAINING PATENTS.

The following is a scale of charges which has been recommended by the Council of the Institute of Patent Agents for adoption by the Fellows of the Institute. These charges are for average cases, and are exclusive of drawings:—

### PROVISIONAL PROTECTION.

Taking instructions for application for Provisional Protection; drawing title, declaration and provisional specification; preparing fair copies, and obtaining Provisional Protection. Paid fee on application £1, and declaration. Agency, letters and postages   ...   ...   ...   ..   ...   ...    £5 5 0

### COMPLETE SPECIFICATION AND PATENT.

Taking instructions for complete specification; drawing and settling complete specification and claims, and preparing fair copies of same; obtaining acceptance of specification, and obtaining Patent. Paid stamp duty on specification £3, and fee on declaration. Agency, letters and postages...   ...   ...    £10 10 0

### WHEN COMPLETE SPECIFICATION IS LODGED IN THE FIRST INSTANCE.

Taking instructions for Protection; drawing and settling title, declaration, complete specification, and claims; preparing fair copies of same; obtaining acceptance of specification and obtaining Patent. Paid stamp duties £4, and fee on declaration. Agency, letters and postages   ...   ...   ...    £12 12 0

# ANALYTICAL SUMMARIES

## OF THE

# PATENT LAWS OF FOREIGN COUNTRIES.

# FOREIGN STATES.

America, United States of.
Argentine Republic.
Austria-Hungary.
Belgium.
Brazil.
Chili.
China.
Colombia, United States of.
Costa Rica.
Denmark.
Ecuador.
Egypt.
Finland.
France.
Germany.
Greece.
Guatemala.

Hawaii.
Hayti.
Holland.
Italy.
Japan.
Liboria.
Luxembourg.
Mexico.
Nicaragua.
Norway.
Portugal.
Russia.
Salvador.
Spain.
Sweden.
Switzerland.
Turkey.
Uruguay.
Venezuela.

# BRITISH COLONIES.

## AUSTRALIA.

New South Wales.
New Zealand.
Queensland.

South Australia.
Tasmania.
Victoria.

Western Australia.

Barbados.
British Guiana.
British Honduras.
Canada.
Cape of Good Hope.
Ceylon.
Fiji.
Gibraltar.
Grenada.
Hong Kong.

India.
Jamaica.
Leeward Islands.
Mauritius.
Natal.
Newfoundland.
St. Lucia.
St. Vincent.
Straits Settlements.
Trinidad.

D

# France.

——o——

France has an area of about 200,000 square miles, and a population of about 38,000,000. The total value of exports in 1880 was about £123,000,000, and the imports for the same year about £163,000,000. The Colonies, to which it is important to note that Patents also extend, consist of Algeria, Senegambia, the Islands of Réunion, Ste. Marie, etc., in the Indian Ocean; also Martinique, Guadaloupe, French Guiana, French Cochin China, New Caledonia, and various others.

The most important manufactures and the places at which they are chiefly carried on in France are:—silk at Lyons, cotton and woollen stuffs at Rouen, Troyes, Lille; woollens at Louviers, Elbœuf, Sédan, Carcassonne, Abbeville, Rheims, Roubaix, etc.; carpets at Paris, Aubusson, Abbeville, and Beauvais; linens (muslin, lace, and gauze) at Lille, Armentières, Valenciennes, Cambrai and St. Quentin; and embroidered articles at Nancy; hardware in the departments of Haute-Marne, Côte-d'Or, Haute-Saône, Ardennes, Niévre, Meuse, Doubs, and Loir-et-Cher; cutlery at Langres, Thiers, and Châtellerault; machinery at Paris, Lille, Nantes, and Creuzot; porcelain at Sèvres, Paris, Limoges, and Bayeux; stoneware at Nevers, Montereau, etc.; common pottery at Paris, Nevers, and Meillonas; beet-root sugar in the department of Nord, and all kinds of fancy and tasteful articles, jewellery, instruments, etc., in Paris. The minerals are exceedingly valuable, and comprise iron, copper, lead, silver, antimony, coal, etc.

The unit of weight is the gramme (=15·432 grains), the unit of capacity 'is the litre (=61·03 cubic inches), and the unit of length is the mètre (=39·37 inches). The multiples of these proceed in decimal progression, and are distinguished by the prefixes *deca, hecto, kilo,* and *myria,* and the subdivisions by *deci, centi,* and *milli.*

The unit of the French monetary system is the franc (about 9½d.) which is divided decimally.

## (*Patent Law of* 1844.)

The law provides for the granting of Patents of Invention, Patents of Improvement, and Certificates of Addition.

**To whom granted.**—Patents are granted to the inventor or his assignee, or to any one legally entitled to the invention, a firm, corporation, &c. In the case of an invention already patented abroad, the foreign patentee has the right to obtain a patent in France, provided the invention has not been published in France or elsewhere.

**For what granted.**—Patents are granted for new industrial products, and new means, or the new application of known means for producing an industrial product or result. Patents are limited to one principal invention, with which may be included any details necessary to fully explain the invention. Pharmaceutical preparations, compositions, or remedies of whatever kind are *not*, however, susceptible of being patented, these being subject to special laws and regulations.

**Novelty of Invention.**—The invention must be new, that is to say, it must not be publicly known either by a published description or by actual practice either in France or elsewhere

**Duration of Patent.**—The maximum duration is 15 years from the date of the application, subject to the payment of an annual tax (see *Taxes*), and also to the conditions hereafter mentioned as to working the invention in France and importing patented articles (see *Conditions of Grant*). The duration of the French patent is also dependent on that of any previous patent obtained elsewhere for the same invention.

**Date of Patent.**—Patents bear date as of the day of filing the application.

**Extent of Grant.**—The patent-right extends to France and to the whole of her Colonies, of which the most important are mentioned above.

**Procedure.**—The application is made by way of a petition to the Minister of Agriculture and Commerce, accompanied by a specification and drawings in duplicate, a memorandum of the documents filed, and a receipt for the first year's tax.

The specification must be in the French language, and contain no other denominations of weights and measures than those mentioned in the patent law of 1844, and the drawings must be made according to a metrical scale.

Applications for patents may be filed at the prefectures of the various departments and in the Colonies, whence they are transmitted to the Ministry of Agriculture and Commerce, in Paris where they are taken up in their order for formal examination.

**Official Examination.**—No official examination is made as to the novelty or utility of the invention. The patent may, however, be refused (*a*) if the application be irregular in form, (*b*) if it contains more than one principal invention, (*c*) if the subject of the invention is unpatentable. In the first two cases the application may be amended, and again presented.

**Taxes.**—Patents are subject to an annual tax of 100 francs, which must be paid prior to the commencement of each year, otherwise the patent will lapse, no grace being allowed for payment.

**Patents of Improvement and Certificates of Addition.**—The inventor or his assignee has, during the term of one year from the date of the original patent, the exclusive right of obtaining a new patent for changes, improvements or additions to the invention which forms the subject of the original patent. Any person, desirous of patenting improvements on an invention already patented by another, may, however, during the currency of the said term of one year lodge an application under seal. At the expiration of the said term the seal will be broken, and a patent issued. But the original patentee will have the right of precedence in respect of any Patent of Improvement or Addition, for any similar changes or improvements, which he may himself have applied for during the same term.

Certificates of Addition are granted only to the original patentee or his assigns during the whole duration of the original patent, for improvements, changes or additions intimately connected with the invention forming the subject of the original patent. Such Certificates of Addition are annexed to, and form part of, the original patent and expire therewith. They are not subject to annual taxes.

**Conditions of Grant; working invention.**—The patent is issued subject to the payment of the annual taxes, and subject to the condition that the invention shall be brought into practical operation in France within two years from the date of signature of the patent (see further condition under *Importation*).  The invention must not cease to be so worked for two consecutive years at a time, unless the patentee can justify his inaction.

A patent is not however cancelled by the omission to work the invention in France, the non-manufacturing being a condition of nullity to take effect only when rendered applicable by a decision of the Courts.  Moreover it must not be too hastily assumed, as is commonly done, that non-compliance with the strict letter of the law, will of necessity render a patent liable to be declared void by the tribunals, for as BÉDARRIDE (an eminent French jurist) remarked in his *Commentaires des lois sur les Brevets d'Invention, etc.*  " The spirit of the law is " indubitable.  It intends only to punish voluntary, premedi- " tated and calculated inactivity," and again " The voidance of " paragraph 2 of Article 32 touches only voluntary inaction. " The law wishes to punish, for inaction, only him who has " willingly remained idle.  It would be really too unjust to " extend the penalty to one who has abstained on account of " circumstances independent of his will."

It would therefore appear that an inventor who takes all steps necessary to ensure the working of his invention, but fails in his attempts from circumstances beyond his control, will run little risk of forfeiting his patent ; but no general rule can be laid down, as the question of non-compliance with the law would be decided by the Courts upon the merits of each particular case.

**Importation and Marking of patented articles.—** The importation of patented articles into France is prohibited under penalty of invalidating the patent.  The Minister of Agriculture, Commerce, and Public Works, may, however, authorize the introduction (*a*) of models of machinery, (*b*) of articles manufactured abroad and intended for public Exhibitions, or for experimental trials made with the concurrence of the Government.

The law imposes no obligation on the patentee to mark patented articles as such, but if they be marked or designated as patented in any advertisement, prospectus, &c., the word " *Breveté* " (which signifies patented) must be followed by the words " *Sans garantie du Gouvernement*," or by the initials *S. G. D. G.*

**Revocation of Patent.**—Patents are liable to be declared invalid (*a*) if the invention was not novel when the patent was applied for; (*b*) if the invention is not susceptible of being patented; (*c*) if the invention relates to principles, methods, systems, or theoretical discoveries, of which no industrial application is specified; (*d*) if the invention is contrary to public morality or safety; (*e*) if the title given falsely indicates something contrary to the nature of the invention; (*f*) if the description is not sufficient to enable the invention to be carried out in practice, and does not comprise the true means that the inventor employs; (*g*) if the invention is not worked in France within the specified time, or if the working ceases for two consecutive years; (*h*) if the patentee imports the patented article into France; and (*i*) if the annual taxes be not duly paid.

**Assignments, &c.**—Patents can be assigned either wholly or in part, and every such assignment must be made by a notarial act in the French language, and must be recorded; but before an assignment will be recorded, the whole of the annual taxes for the residue of the term of the patent must be paid.

Until the assignment is recorded it will possess no legal value.

**Infringements.**—The penalty for infringing the patent either by the manufacture of the products of the invention, or by the employment of the means patented, or by vending or exposing the products for sale, or by introducing the same into France, is from 100 to 2000 francs, to which may be added, in certain cases, a term of imprisonment not exceeding 6 months.

# Belgium.

—o—

Belgium is one of the smallest of the European states, comprising nine provinces, viz., Antwerp, Brabant, West Flanders, East Flanders, Hainault, Liege, Luneburg, Luxemburg, and Namur. Though its territory is very limited compared with the great European States, being under 12,000 square miles, its agricultural and commercial importance is considerable. The population of Belgium in 1880 was nearly 5¼ millions. The manufactures of Belgium are very important, and many are superior to those of other countries, the principal exports being wrought iron, hardware, machinery, linens, woollens, cottons, yarns, sugar, paper, glass, fire-arms, lace. The linens of Flanders and lace of South Brabant have a special reputation. Carpets and porcelain are produced at Tournay, cloth at Verviers, carriages at Brussels, cutlery at Namur, beet-root sugar in Hainault and Antwerp. There are very extensive foundries and machine works at Charleroi and Liege.

*(Patent Law of 24th May, 1854.)*

Patents of Invention and Patents of Importation (which confer the same rights as Patents of Invention) are granted according as the invention is first patented in Belgium or in some other country. Patents of Improvement are also granted to the original patentee and to others for subsequent improvements on, or additions to, a previously patented invention.

**To whom granted.**—Patents are granted to the inventor or his assignee duly appointed, or any one legally entitled to the invention, a company, &c. A simple power from the inventor, authorising any one to take a Belgian Patent in his own name, is sufficient, said power being stamped and registered.

**For what granted.**—Patents are granted for all discoveries or improvements that may be worked as articles of industry and commerce.

**Novelty of Invention**.—The invention must not have been worked commercially by others than the inventor within the Kingdom of Belgium prior to the date of application for the patent. The working by the inventor himself before the application for a patent does not, therefore, necessarily affect its validity. The publication in Belgium of the blue-book of the English specification, prior to the date of application for the Belgian patent, does not prejudice the latter, but a complete printed description and drawings must not have been published in Belgium (otherwise than by a legal formality) prior to the application for the Belgian patent. Subject to these conditions a foreign patentee, though his patent be several years old, may obtain a valid Belgian Patent of Importation, and should any Belgian patent for the same invention have been taken out by another person subsequent to the date of his foreign patent, he may apply to the Courts to confirm his rights in priority to such other patentee.

**Duration of Patent**.—The duration of a Patent of Invention (granted for an invention which has not been patented elsewhere) is 20 years. The duration of a Patent of Importation (granted for an invention first patented in some other country) is limited to that of the previous foreign patent of longest term. The duration is in all cases subject to the conditions hereafter mentioned as to payment of taxes (see *Taxes*) and working the invention (see *Conditions of Grant*).

**Date of Patent**.—The patent bears date as of the day of filing the application.

**Extent of Grant**.—The patent extends to the whole Kingdom of Belgium.

**Procedure**.—The application is made by depositing a petition on stamped paper indicating the date and duration of the original foreign patent (if any), and accompanied by a full and complete specification, and drawings in duplicate, a memorandum of the documents, and a receipt for the first year's tax. The specification must clearly describe the invention,

and point out its essential features. It must be written either
in the French, Flemish or German language, and if in either
of the two latter must be accompanied by a French translation
when the applicant is not resident in Belgium. All specifications must be written without interlineations; all words struck
out must be initialled and counted. If the petitioner be the
assignee of the inventor, an assignment, or a simple power
stamped and registered, authorizing the assignee to take the
patent in his own name, is required.

**Official Examination.**—No examination is made as to
the novelty or utility of the invention.

**Taxes.**—Patents of Invention, and Patents of Importation
are subject to the payment of a small annual tax increasing
progressively at the rate of 10 francs per annum, a month's
grace being allowed subject to a fine of 10 francs. Patents of
Improvement are exempt from taxes when granted to the
owner of the original patent.

**Patents of Improvement.**—Patents of Improvement
are granted to the original patentee; they are exempt from
taxes, and expire with the original patent. The Patent of
Improvement must be for improvements of the same nature as
the original invention, otherwise it will not be held legally
valid. Patents of Improvement are also granted to others than
the owner of the original patent, but in that case they are
subject to the same taxes as original patents, and the holder
of the Patent of Improvement cannot use the invention without
the license of the owner of the original patent and conversely.

**Conditions of Grant; working invention.**—The
invention must be brought into practical operation in Belgium
within one year of its having been worked elsewhere, and whilst
continuing to be worked abroad, must not cease to be so worked
in Belgium for an entire year at a time, unless the grantee can
justify his inaction. It is not considered sufficient to import
the articles from abroad and sell them in Belgium; nor is it a
strict compliance with the spirit of the law to make a few in

Belgium whilst importing largely from abroad and selling in Belgium, but the law is very indefinite and lax on this question.

**Importation and Marking of patented articles.** —The introduction of patented articles by the patentee is not prohibited, and the law imposes no obligation to mark patented articles as such.

**Revocation of Patent.**—Patents lapse by non-payment of the annual taxes within the prescribed time, and are liable to be annulled (*a*) for neglect to work the invention in Belgium within the prescribed period, and thereafter continuously; (*b*) for want of novelty (see *Novelty of Invention*); (*c*) for insufficiency of specification.

**Assignments, etc.**—Every assignment and license must be notified to the proper department, and an authentic copy of the deed must be furnished.

# Germany.

——o——

The most important manufactures and the places where they are carried on are as follows—linen in Prussian Silesia, Saxony and Westphalia: cotton in Alsace-Lorraine, Wurtemburg, and the Grand Duchy of Baden ; silk in the Rhine Provinces and in Baden ; iron in most of the States, but principally in Prussia, Alsace-Lorraine, Bavaria, and Saxony; and steel in the Rhine Provinces. Other manufactures are beet-root sugar, leather, porcelain, musical instruments, &c. Breweries and distilleries are to be met with everywhere. The money, weights, and measures are now uniform throughout the Empire. The denominational unit of the monetary system is the Mark (about equal to 1s.) which is divided into 100 pfennige. Since January, 1872, the French metrical system of weights and measures has been in force. A measure equal to half a litre is called a schoppen, and one equal to 50 litres is called a scheffel. Half a kilogramme is 1 pfund ; 50 kilogrammes or 100 pfund make 1 centner ; and 1000 kilogrammes make 1 tonne. The population in 1880 was upwards of 45,000,000.

---

### (*Patent Law of* 1877.)

Patents of Invention are granted, and also Patents of Addition for improvements on previously patented inventions.

**To whom granted.**—Patents are granted to the first applicant, whether he be the inventor or merely the importer. The patent may be taken in the name of a company or firm.

**For what granted.**—Patents are granted for new inventions which admit of industrial use, but not for articles of food, drinks, and medicines, nor for substances produced by a chemical method, if the invention does not relate to the method of producing such articles.

**Novelty of Invention.**—The invention must not have been described in a printed publication in any country, nor publicly worked in Germany prior to the date of application for the patent.

**Duration of Patent.**—The duration of the patent is **15** years, subject to the payment of the annual taxes (see *Taxes*), and to the conditions as to working the invention and granting licenses hereafter mentioned (see *Conditions of Grant*). The duration of the German patent is not affected by the lapsing of prior foreign patents for the same invention.

**Date of Patent.**—The date from which the duration of the patent runs is the day following the filing of the application.

**Extent of Grant.**—The patent extends to the whole Empire of Germany, that is to say, the Kingdoms of Prussia, Saxony, Wurtemburg, Bavaria, the Territory of Alsace-Lorraine, and all the minor States.

**Procedure.**—The application for a patent is made by a petition, accompanied by a specification in the German language, a drawing on cardboard (of certain dimensions), and a duplicate drawing on tracing cloth. Measures and weights must be quoted according to the metrical system, temperatures according to the Celsius scale, and densities as specific weights. If the application is approved by the Patent Office, provisional protection is accorded in the first instance, and a notification thereof is officially published. Objections to the grant may be lodged within eight weeks from the date of this publication.

**Official Examination.**—An official examination is made by an examiner as to the novelty of the invention before the patent is granted. In case of an adverse decision an appeal may be lodged within four weeks, and a further term is allowed for stating the grounds of the appeal. The appeal is heard by another examiner, whose decision is final.

**Model.**—In ordinary cases no model is required, but when necessary for due examination of the invention a model is called for. When the invention relates to improvements in firearms, a specimen or working model must be supplied to the Patent Office. Models of spools, spindles, shuttles, and skates must also be supplied. These are retained by the Patent Office if the patent be granted.

**Taxes.**—Patents are subject to a progressively increasing annual tax (for the payment of which three months' grace is allowed) commencing at 50 marks and increasing by 50 marks in each subsequent year.

**Certificates of Addition.**—Patents or Certificates of Addition are granted for improvements on an invention already patented. Such supplementary patents are exempt from annual taxes, and terminate with the original patent.

**Conditions of Grant; working invention.**—The invention must be worked in Germany to an adequate extent within three years from the date of the patent, or at least everything must be done to ensure its being worked. It is advisable to obtain a certificate proving compliance with this requirement of the law, for use in case of litigation. If from the nature of the case it is found impossible to put the invention into practical operation within the specified time, it is well to publish advertisements or announce in some way that the patentee is desirous either of disposing of the patent or of granting licences, so that it may in case of necessity be shown that the patentee has made *bonâ fide* attempts to have the invention worked in the Empire. The patent is subject also to the payment of the taxes above mentioned (see *Taxes*), and to the obligation to grant licenses under certain circumstances (see *Compulsory Licenses*).

**Importation and Marking of patented articles.**—The law does not prohibit the importation by the patentee of articles made in accordance with the patent, and imposes no obligation to mark patented articles as such, but it is recommended that they should be marked with the words " *Deutsches Reichs Patent*," or with the initials *D. R. P.*, followed in either case by the date of the patent, but the article must not be so marked until the grant is finally allowed. The fraudulent marking of articles is punishable by fine or imprisonment.

**Revocation of Patent.**—The patent will be annulled if

it is found that the invention was not patentable, or that the essential parts of the invention were taken from another person without consent.　The patent will be revoked for non-working of the invention within the prescribed time (see *Conditions of Grant)*, and also in case of the patentee refusing to grant licenses required in the public interest upon adequate compensation. The patent lapses by non-payment of the taxes within the prescribed time (see *Taxes*).

**Assignments, &c.**—Assignments of German Patents must be registered in Germany in order to be legally valid, and for this purpose an assignment executed by the assignor, and a declaration of acceptance executed by the assignee, must be lodged at the Patent Office; the signatures to both documents must be certified by a notary and legalised by the German Consul.

**Compulsory Licenses.**—In case of licenses being required for the public interest, the patentee is bound to grant such licenses upon adequate compensation, under penalty of revocation of the patent.

# United States of America.

—o—

The area of the United States, exclusive of Alaska, is about 3,000,000 square miles, and the population in 1880 was upwards of 50,000,000. The chief manufactures, and the localities where they are carried on, are as follows:—cotton in Massachusetts, Pennsylvania, Rhode Island, Connecticut and New York; woollen goods in the above-mentioned States, and also in New Hampshire, Vermont, Ohio and California: iron in Philadelphia, Pittsburg, Cincinnati, New York, Baltimore and St. Louis; boots and shoes by machinery in Massachusetts. Other manufactures are leather, railway and tramway cars, hardware, cutlery, agricultural implements, labour-saving machinery, &c., steam engines, petroleum and other oils, paper, musical instruments, sugar, flour, and other food products, hosiery, india-rubber goods, and others too numerous to mention.

The exports in 1881 were upwards of 902,000,000 dollars, and the imports 642,000,000 dollars.

Accounts are kept in dollars (one dollar is equal to about four shillings) and cents. The weights and measures are the same as in Great Britain.

---

(*Patent Law of July 8th,* 1870, *as revised in the General Revision of Federal Statutes in* 1874.)

Patents for Inventions are granted for 17 years, subject, however, when the invention has been previously patented elsewhere, to the condition that the American patent shall be limited to the term for which such previous foreign patent was granted.

**To whom granted.**—Patents are granted to the original and first inventor, or his assignee, or to the inventor and assignee conjointly. If the invention result from the joint action of two or more minds, the patent must be taken conjointly by the co-inventors.

**For what granted.**—Patents are granted for any new and useful art, machine, manufacture, or composition of matter, or any new and useful improvement therein. The invention must be the result of ingenuity, or the production of inventive faculty, in contra-distinction to the mere novel employment of a known machine or apparatus. It is essential that it should be useful, and not contrary to morality, nor harmful. The patent is strictly limited to a single invention.

**Novelty of Invention.**—In the case of inventions which have been already patented in England or elsewhere, the publication in the United States of the English or foreign specification does not deprive the invention of the attribute of novelty. The only restriction is that the invention must not have been put in public use nor on sale in the United States for more than two years prior to the application.

**Duration of Patent.**—The duration of the patent is seventeen years from date of issue of the patent except when the invention has been previously patented abroad, in which case the American patent will expire with the term for which the foreign patent was nominally granted. If there be more than one previous foreign patent, the life of the American patent will be limited to the one nominally granted for the shortest term.

**Date of Patent.**—The Letters Patent are dated as of the day of issue.

**Extent of Grant.**—The patent extends to the United States and the territories thereof.

**Procedure.**—Formal application is made by filing a complete specification with drawings in all cases capable of illustration together with petition and oath, and if the documents be in correct order the case is taken up for examination. The application must be completed and prepared for examination within two years from date of filing, and in default thereof, or upon failure of the applicant to prosecute the same within two years after any action thereon, the application will be regarded as abandoned, unless it be satisfactorily shown that such delay was unavoidable. But such abandonment will not prevent the filing of a new application for the same invention.

**Model.**—None is required, unless the same shall be called for by the examiner.

**Official Examination.**—A rigorous examination is made as to the patentability and novelty of the invention by examiners, from whose decision if adverse to the grant of the patent, an appeal may be made in succession to a Board of Examiners in chief, to the Commissioner of Patents, to the Supreme Court of the District of Columbia, and finally by bill in equity before any United States Court.

**Taxes.**—Patents are not subject to any taxes or further payments after the issue of the patent.

**Objections or Interferences.**—Interference proceedings or claims to priority of invention may be entered by others claiming the same invention, and although the Commissioner has no power to cancel a patent, he may grant a second patent for the same invention to another person after such person has established by evidence in due form his priority of invention Interferences are also declared by the office both when the same invention is claimed by two or more original applicants, and in certain other cases. An applicant may, in order to avoid the continuance of the interference, disclaim the particular matter in issue, such disclaimer forming part of his specification.

The grant of a patent to a fraudulent applicant will not be a bar to the right of the original and first inventor to obtain a patent for the invention subsequently.

**Conditions of Grant ; working invention.**—The law imposes no obligation on the patentee to practice his invention within any specified time.

**Importation and Marking of patented articles.**—The importation by the patentee of the articles patented by him is not prohibited.

Every article made under a patent must be marked "Patented," with the date of the patent, or if the character of the article renders this impracticable, the wrapper, package, or label must be so marked. The only penalty for failure to mark

E

is that no damages can be recovered for any involuntary in-fringements, but only for those committed after the infringer has been specially notified of the existence of the patent. But if the infringer knew that a patent existed, then he is liable although the article was not marked patented.

**Re-issues and Disclaimers.**—A re-issue, which is a new and corrected patent issued in place of a defective one which has been surrendered, is granted to the patentee, his legal representatives, or the assignees of the entire interest, when by reason of a defective or insufficient specification, or by reason of a patentee claiming more than he had a right to claim, the patent is invalid, provided that the error has arisen from inadvertence, accident, or mistake, and without fraud or deceptive intention.

The re-issue must, however, be applied for within reasonable time after the issue of the patent.

Disclaimers may be applied for, when the patent can be cor-rected by simply erasing a certain claim or a certain clause in the specification, but when the specification or claims require to be re-written in any part, a re-issue must be applied for.

**Assignments and Licences.**—Inventors may assign their rights either wholly or in part, and either before or after the grant is issued. The assignment may extend to the whole term of the patent or to part only, and may be limited to certain counties, states, &c.

Assignments must be recorded within three months of their date, or they will not be valid against a subsequent purchaser in good faith.

If the inventor assign his rights before the grant of the patent, the latter can be issued jointly to the inventor and his assignees or to the latter only, according to the terms of the assignment.

Joint owners of a patent are not partners. Each owner of an undivided share in a patent may work the invention, and sell rights under his share to others without accounting to the other owners of the patent.

**Joint Owners.**—Joint inventors are joint owners of a patent the same as joint assignees. Unless there be some proof to the contrary, joint owners are assumed to be equal owners. Either can manufacture, use, and sell his share or parts thereof without accounting to the other, can grant a non-exclusive license under the patent, and assign his interest independently of his co-owner.

Damages for infringements must, however, be divided between the owners in proportion of their respective interests.

# Spain.

---0---

This Kingdom comprises with the Balearic and Canary Islands, an area of about 196,000 square miles. Population in 1879 about 17,000,000. The colonies and dependencies of this kingdom are the West Indian islands of Cuba and Porto Rico, the Phillipine Islands in the Indian seas, the African possessions in the Gulf of Guinea, and Fernando Po. The population of these colonies is about 8,300,000. Spain itself is rich in minerals, including gold, silver, quicksilver, lead, copper, iron, calamine, coal, &c. In recent years manufactures have to some extent revived, more especially in cotton-spinning and weaving, paper-making, soap, leather, and metal industries. The chief industrial centres are the provinces of Barcelona, Gerona, Tarragona, Guipuzcoa, and Biscay.

Accounts are kept in centimos and pesetas. 100 centimos (one peseta), equal to 9½d. Average rate of exchange, 25 pesetas for £1. The weights and measures are the same as in France, but the old weights are sometimes employed, of which the principal are—the quintal (100 libras), equal to 101·4 lbs. avoir.; the arroba (for wine), 3½ imperial gallons—(for oil), 2¾ imperial gallons; the fanega, 1½ imperial bushels.

In the colony of Cuba, rice, sugar and tobacco are produced, the latter two being the most important crops. Porto Rico is almost an agricultural island, the products being the same as those of Cuba, and tobacco and coffee the largest exports. In the Phillippine Island's sugar, rice, indigo, coffee, cotton, &c., are produced.

---

## (*Patent Law of* 1878.)

Patents of Invention, Patents of Introduction, and Certificates of Addition are granted for 20 years and under. (See *Duration.*)

**To whom granted.**—Patents are granted to the inventor or importer, whether an individual, firm, or company. For the different terms of patents granted to inventors and importers see under *Duration.*

**For what granted.**—Patents are granted for machinery, apparatus, instruments, processes, or mechanical or chemical operations, being entirely or partly new and peculiar, or which, without these attributes, have not been established or executed in the same way or form in the Spanish dominions. Also new industrial products or results, obtained by new or known means, provided their working forms a new branch of industry in the country; but patents relating to such products or results shall not prevent others from using the objects mentioned previously for obtaining the same products or results.

Patents are granted for:—(*a*) the result or product of apparatus or processes first above mentioned, provided they are not contained in the second part of the paragraph; (*b*) the use of natural products; (*c*) scientific principles or discoveries of a speculative nature, not applicable to machinery or processes; (*d*) pharmaceutical operations or medicines; (*e*) financial schemes.

**Novelty of Invention.**—The invention must not have been known or worked in the Spanish dominions or abroad, in the case of a 20 years patent. (See under *Duration*, for patents of shorter term.)

**Duration of Patent.**—For inventions not published either in Spain or elsewhere 20 years. The duration of the patent is not affected by the lapsing of prior foreign patents for the same invention. For inventions already patented and published elsewhere, 10 years, provided the application be made in Spain within two years from the date of the foreign patent. For inventions which are not original (*i.e.*, the invention of the applicant), or which, being original, are not new in Spain or elsewhere, five years. The term is computed from the date of the patent, which is generally three or four months after filing the application, but priority is acquired from the date of filing the application. The patent, for whatever term it may be granted, is subject to the payment of taxes (see *Taxes*) and other conditions mentioned below. (See *Conditions of Grant*).

**Date of Patent.**—The patent is generally dated from one to two months later than the concession or grant.

**Extent of Grant.**—The patent extends to Spain and the islands adjacent, and all the colonies.

**Procedure.**—The application is made by a petition on stamped paper addressed to the Civil Governor of the province, accompanied by a duplicate specification (in Spanish) and drawings (also in duplicate) on tracing cloth, a power of attorney, and stamped paper representing the first year's tax, and an officially certified memorandum of the documents. The documents are deposited in the office of the Civil Governor, whence they are passed to the " Conservatorio," where they are examined and reported on, and are afterwards sent to the Minister of Public Works. If the application is in order the patent is then conceded, and ultimately is returned from the Ministry of Public Works to the " Conservatorio"; the diploma is then signed by the Minister, and duly registered in the Patent Office. All application relating to patents, whether new or existing, must be made through the Civil Governor of the province for the time being.

**Official Examination.**—There is no examination either as to the novelty or to the utility of the invention.

**Taxes.**—The patent is subject to an annual and progressive tax commencing at 10 pesetas and increasing at the rate of 10 pesetas per annum.

**Certificates of Addition.**—Certificates of addition are delivered (with the same formalities as an original patent) for improvements upon the subject of the original patent, the protection thereby acquired terminating with the original patent. The annual taxes on the original patent cover the certificates of addition annexed thereto.

**Conditions of Grant ; working invention.** — The invention must be worked in Spain within two years from the date of the patent, and the working must be officially certified. Moreover the working must not be interrupted for more than a year at any subsequent time, unless the owner can show good cause for the interruption.

**Importation and Marking of patented articles.**— The law does not prohibit the importation by the patentee of the patented articles into Spain, and does not impose any obligation on the patentee to mark the patented articles as such.

**Revocation of Patent.**—Patents are declared void by failure to pay the annual taxes; for breach of the conditions as to working the invention within the specified time ; and they may be annulled at the instance of third parties, and by the sentence of a Spanish Court upon proof that the invention was not new when the patent was applied for, or that the specification insufficiently describes how the invention is to be worked, and upon other grounds.

**Amendments and Disclaimers.**—The law does not provide for amending specifications except by way of certificate of addition.

**Infringements.**—Infringements of patents are punishable by fine, damages, and the confiscation of the counterfeit articles to the patentee.

**Assignments.**—All assignments or modifications of the original right must be registered at Madrid. The deeds must be in Spanish, or must be officially translated and legalised. The payment of. the annual taxes up to the date of the contract must be proved and various other formalities observed.

# Italy.

——o——

The Kingdom of Italy includes the Islands of Sicily and Sardinia, to which Letters Patent also extend. Manufactures have in recent years made great progress, especially in Tuscany and the northern provinces. The most important is silk spinning, in which Italy excels. Woollen manufactures are chiefly carried on in Upper Italy. The linen and hemp manufactures are also important. Cotton manufactures are chiefly carried on in Lombardy. A good deal of machinery is constructed in Liguria. Lombardy stands at the head of the iron industry. Boracic acid is an important product. Tartaric acid, citric acid, the manufacture of soap, and the preparation of alizarine, may also be particularly mentioned. Population in 1871 about 27,000,000. Accounts are kept in lire (9½d.) and centesimi (⅒d).

———————————

*(Patent Laws of 1859 and 1864 and Decree of 1870.)*

Patents of Invention and Patents of Importation (which confer the same rights as Patents of Invention) are granted according as the invention is first patented in Italy or in some other country.

Certificates of Addition are also issued.

**To whom granted.**—Patents are granted to the inventor, and in the case of an invention already patented abroad, to the inventor or his assigns. Applications may be made by individuals, corporations, firms, or associations, &c.

**For what granted.**—Patents are granted for any new invention having for its immediate object—(*a*) an industrial product or result ; (*b*) an instrument, machine, tool, or mechanical apparatus ; (*c*) a process or mode of manufacture ; (*d*) a motor, or the application of any known force to industrial purposes ; (*e*) and lastly, the practical application of a scientific principle in such a manner as to directly produce industrial results, in which case the patent is limited solely to the results specified. But inventions that relate to anything contrary to law, morals, or public safety, or that do not relate to the manufacture of material objects, or that are of a mere theoretical nature, and medicines, are not patentable. Inventions relating to alimentary substances are referred to the Superior Board of Health, and if thought injurious the patent is refused The patent is limited to a single invention.

**Novelty of Invention.**—An invention is considered new, if not already so completely within public knowledge in Italy as to enable any person to put it in practice. An invention already patented abroad, although it may have been published by the patent, is still considered new, provided that the invention has not been freely imported and worked in the Kingdom by other parties prior to the application for the Italian patent and provided that the foreign patent be still in force.

**Duration of Patent.**—The maximum duration of the patent is fifteen years, subject to the payment of annual taxes (see *Taxes*), and to certain conditions as to working the invention (see *Conditions of Grant*). In the case of an invention already patented abroad, the Italian patent expires with the foreign patent of longest term, provided it does not exceed fifteen years. Patents may be granted for any number of years from one to fifteen, and may be prolonged from year to year until the maximum term is reached. It is usual to apply for a six years patent, for the reason mentioned under *Conditions of Grant*.

**Date of Patent.**—The duration of the patent is computed from the last day of the quarter of the year in which the application is made, but priority is acquired and the patent takes effect with respect to third parties from the date of application.

**Extent of Grant.**—The patent extends to the whole Kingdom of Italy including the islands of Sicily and Sardinia.

**Procedure.**—The application must contain, besides formal particulars, a description (in triplicate) of the invention in French or Italian on stamped paper; drawings (in triplicate, and made to the smallest possible metrical scale); a receipt for the taxes corresponding to the term of the patent applied for; a legalised power of attorney; a memorandum of the documents, and in the case of a Patent of Importation, the original foreign patent or a legalised copy. If the application be made by the assignee of the foreign patentee a proper assignment must be produced.

**Official Examination.**—A formal examination is made of the documents and as to the patentability of the invention, but none as to its novelty and utility.

**Taxes.**—The patent is subject to two kinds of taxes, viz., a proportional and an annual tax.

The proportional tax is equal to 10 lire multiplied by the number of years applied for, whether on an original application or by way of prolongation of a patent already granted, and is payable in advance.

The annual tax is 40 lire for the 1st, 2nd, and 3rd years, and increases 25 lire at triennial intervals.

Each prolongation of a patent of a short term is subject to an extra tax of 40 lire, besides the proportional and annual taxes above mentioned. Three months grace is allowed for payment of the annual taxes.

**Certificates of Addition.**—Certificates of addition are granted to the patentee or his assigns for improvements on the patented invention, which improvements are thereby protected for the residue of the term of the original patent with which they are prolonged and expire, the taxes on the original patent covering also the certificates of addition annexed thereto. Applications for such certificates of addition made by the patentee or his assignee during the first six months of the duration of the patent take precedence over similar applications made by other parties.

**Conditions of Grant; working.**—Patents granted for six years and upwards must be brought into practical operation in Italy within two years from the date of the patent, and such working must not, at any subsequent time, be discontinued for two consecutive years. For patents granted for shorter terms the limitation is one year in each case.   The patentee does not however, necessarily forfeit his rights by failure to comply with these conditions, if due to causes beyond his control.   Want of pecuniary means is not, however, a valid excuse.   It is advisable to have the working of the invention legally proved by a notarial certificate.

**Importation and Marking of patented articles.**—The law does not prohibit the importation by the patentee of the patented articles, and does not impose any obligation to mark the patented articles as such.

**Revocation of Patent.**—Patents are void if the invention is unpatentable ; if granted for alimentary substances against the advice of the Board of Health ; if the title indicates falsely the object of the invention ; if the specification is insufficient ; if the invention is not new or useful in industry ; if the invention is a modification of another patent of less than six months prior date; if the taxes be not paid in due time ; if the invention is not worked within the prescribed time.

**Disclaimers.**—Certificates of reduction (which are equivalent to disclaimers) may be entered only during the first six months of a patent.   The application must distinctly point out the parts to be disclaimed, and must be accompanied by a new specification and drawings in triplicate, to be substituted for those originally filed, and by the payment of 40 lire.

**Assignments.**—Every assignment must be on stamped paper and in the French or Italian language, and must be registered at the Ministry and published in the Official Gazette at the expense of the applicant, and is not valid with respect to third parties until so registered.   The original deed and a memorandum in duplicate of certain formal particulars must be produced, of which the former will be returned.   In case of a total assignment, the assignees are bound to pay the taxes, but in case of a partial assignment, the deed cannot be registered until all the taxes have been paid up for the remainder of the term of the patent.

**Infringements.**—The infringement of a patent by manufacturing, selling, or importing, is punishable by a fine not exceeding 500 lire and by seizure of the counterfeit objects and
·apparatus used in their manufacture, besides damages.

# Austria-Hungary.

———0———

The Austrian Empire, which is the largest State next to Russia on the continent of Europe, is divided into two great sections, one being composed of the Austrian, or Cisleithan provinces, and the other of the Transleithan provinces, or lands of the Hungarian Crown. The Empire embraces an area of upwards of 240 000 square miles, and has a population, according to the census of 1880, of about 38,000,000, without taking into account the Turkish provinces of Bosnia and Herzegovina, which are now administered by Austria. Manufactures flourish most in Bohemia, Moravia, Silesia, Lower Austria, and Vorarlberg.

The chief articles produced are—cotton, woollen and linen goods, leather, articles of silver, iron and steel, glass, and earthenware. In the manufacture of scientific instruments, Austria holds a high position. The iron industry has recently developed to a considerable extent, and in the manufacture of machinery great advances have been made. In Bohemia and Moravia sugar is produced from beet to a large extent. The manufacture of leather goods is also very large.

Accounts in Austria are kept in gulden, or florins of 100 neukreutzer each. The florin is equal to about 2s. The centner, by which all considerable weights are calculated, is equal to 123½lbs. avoir. The metz is equal to 1·7 imperial bushel. The eimer (the customary liquid measure) is equal to 14·94 English wine gallons. The Vienna foot is equal to 12·45 inches.

———————

## (Patent Law.)

On the establishment of the dual system of government in Austria-Hungary, it was decided by a special agreement between the ministers of Hungary and Cisleithania, that the Imperial Decree of 15th August, 1852, in which the law and practice with regard to inventions are fully explained, should remain in force throughout the whole empire.

In accordance with the terms of this agreement, the Cisleithanian and Hungarian Ministers of Commerce submit to mutual approval the inventions for which they intend granting patents, and subsequently to such approval each ministry issues patents, bearing identical dates, for its respective division of the empire.

Thus, an inventor, desirous of securing an exclusive right to his invention in Austria-Hungary, must provide himself with two patents. These are, however, granted on a single application, addressed, at the choice of the applicant, either to the Cisleithanian or Hungarian Ministry of Commerce, and on one payment of the fees.

The patents thus issued are likewise valid in Bosnia and Herzegovina. They are granted either as *secret* patents or *public* patents. In the case of a secret patent the documents are not open to · public inspection during the existence of the patent in its secret form, and damages for infringements cannot be obtained, until the infringer has been officially informed of the existence of the patent, and the object of the invention, by a notary or legal functionary; but an injunction may be obtained and an order for the seizure or destruction of the counterfeit articles. It is customary to apply for a secret patent, thereby avoiding publication until all foreign patents are secured. A secret patent may, on application at any subsequent time be declared public, but public patents must always remain open t.» inspection.

**To whom granted.**—In the case of inventions patented elsewhere, Austrian patents are only granted to the original patentee or his legal assignee during the existence of the foreign patent. A foreigner can however obtain a patent in Austria whether a foreign patent has or has not been obtained. But if the invention patented abroad has been worked abroad before application is made for the Austrian patent, it is necessary to produce the foreign patent, upon which the Austrian will be founded, and on the life of which it will depend.

**For what granted.**—Patents are granted for any new discovery, invention, or improvement, having for object a new industrial product or new means or method of production, but not for alimentary preparations, beverages or medicines, nor for methods of preparing the same, nor for scientific principles or theories. A part of a process of manufacturing articles of food, beverages, and medicines, may however be patented; thus for instance many inventions relating to the manufacture of sugar, beer, etc., are patented.

**Novelty of Invention.**—Inventions are considered new when they have not been worked in the Empire or described in a printed publication prior to the date of application for the patent.

**Duration of Patent.**—Patents are granted for any number of years not exceeding 15. They are usually obtained for one year, with power of renewal to 15 years by application for prolongation and payment of annual taxes (see *Taxes*), and the production of the original patent at the time of each payment. The duration of the patent runs from the day of signature of the patent, and is subject to the condition mentioned below as to working the invention (see *Conditions of Grant*), and is limited by the life of the previous foreign patent for the same invention, if such foreign patent was previously worked abroad, and was produced at the application.

**Date of Patent.**—The date from which the duration of the patent runs is the date of grant or signature, but priority is acquired from the time of filing the application. The patent is generally issued about one month after the grant.

**Extent of Grant.**—The Empire of Austria and the Kingdom of Hungary, together with Bosnia and Herzegovina. ·

**Procedure.**—The application is made by filing a specification in the German language and drawings (all in duplicate) at the Ministry of Commerce in Vienna, accompanied by a legalised power of attorney. The application is referred to the Polytechnical Institute of Vienna for examination of the documents, and as to the patentability of the invention. If objections are raised, the applicant is informed thereof, and time allowed for amending the specification. If the invention be of an unpatentable character the patent is refused. If no objection be raised the documents are then sent to the Hungarian Ministry of Commerce, Budapest, where a second examination is made. If no objection be made by the Polytechnical School of Budapest, the Hungarian patent is granted, registered, and sent to Vienna, where the Austrian patent is granted under the same date as in Hungary, and the dual patent issued to the applicant, the specification being then opened to public inspection or kept secret in the archives, according as a public or a secret patent has been applied for.

**Official Examination.**—The documents are examined as to the sufficiency of the specification and the patentability of the invention generally, but no examination is made as to the novelty and utility of the invention before the grant of the patent.

**Taxes.**—Patents granted for less than fifteen years may be prolonged to that extent by special application for renewal, and by the payment of an annual tax or prolongation fee commencing at 26 florins for each of the first five years and thereafter increasing progressively.

**Conditions of Grant ; working.**—The invention must be worked in Austria within one year from the date of the patent, and it is advisable to have such working officially certified. The working must not be subsequently discontinued for two consecutive years.

**Importation and Marking of patented articles.**—The importation of the patented articles from abroad by the patentee does not affect the validity of the Austrian patent.

The law imposes no obligation to mark the patented articles as such.

**Revocation of Patent.**—Patents may be cancelled on proof that the specification is insufficient or that the invention was not new in the Empire at the date of application for the patent, or that the invention is identical with that for which a previous Austrian patent has been granted; also, in the case of a foreign invention, on the ground that the patentee is not the owner of the foreign patent, if the invention has been worked abroad before application in Austria ; also for non-working of the invention within the prescribed time, or interruption of the working during two consecutive years. A patent granted for less than 15 years lapses by efflux of time, unless subsequently renewed by the payment of the annual taxes or prolongation fees.

**Assignments and Licenses.**—Assignments, etc., must be officially legalised and registered in Austria.

**Infringements.**—Infringements of patent rights are :—

(*a*) The imitation of the products of a patented invention even when such imitation results from the possession of a subsequent or partially identical patent.

(*b*) The importation for sale of counterfeit products.

(*c*) The sale, exhibition, etc., of such products.

A first infringement of a *public* patent, a second one of a *secret* patent, is punishable with a fine varying from 25 fl. to 1,000 fl., and on non-payment of the same, by one day's arrest for every 5 fl. of the fine imposed, and by confiscation of the machinery, tools, etc.

# Portugal.

———o———

This Kingdom has an area of 34,501 square miles. The population in 1878 was about 5,000,000. The foreign possessions of Portugal consist of Goa, Damaun, Diu, etc., in Hindustan, Macao, in the Indian Archipelago, Cape Verde, St. Thomas and Prince's Islands, Guinea, Angola, Mozambique, the Island of Madeira, the Azores, etc. In Madeira, sugar cane has, since the outbreak of the vine disease some time ago, received considerable attention. In Portugal manufactures are very limited in extent, but have increased of late years. Woollen cloth and other woollen stuffs are made at Portalegre and Alemquer; delft and ordinary earthenware at Lisbon, Oporto, Coimbra, Caldas, Beja, Estremoz, etc.; prints at Lisbon and Oporto; lace at Peniche; cotton twist at Thomar; silks at Braganza, Chacim, Oporto, etc.; copper and tinware at Lisbon, etc. Shipbuilding is also well understood, and a few vessels are constructed at Lisbon, Figueira, Oporto, and Villa do Conde. The mineral products are of considerable importance, and comprise manganese, lead, copper, iron, coal, salt, etc. Wine is the chief export. Accounts are kept in reis and milreis or 1000 reis. The value of the real is so small that the milreis is worth only about 4s. 4½d. The French metric system was introduced about 1860.

## (*Patent Law of* 1868 *and* 1870.)

Patents of Invention are granted under the Royal Sign Manual, and Certificates of Addition are also granted for improvements on inventions already patented.

**To whom granted.**—Patents are granted to the true and first inventor, either by himself or his duly authorised agent. The patent may also be taken by a society or company, and by natives or aliens, but not by a mere importer who is not the actual inventor.

**For what granted.**—Patents are granted for all inventions, discoveries or improvements on machines, apparatus, processes, systems, or commercial products, possessing the character of novelty and utility, providing they do not relate to illegal or immoral objects. A valid patent cannot however be obtained either for an invention already known in Portugal either practically or theoretically, by a technical description in a Portuguese or foreign work or by other means, or for changes which do not possess utility, but merely consist of alterations in form or proportion or simply in ornamentation.

**Novelty of Invention.**—The invention must be new in the Kingdom of Portugal.

**Duration of Patent.**—The maximum term granted is 15 years, and the patent is delivered for one, two, three or more years, as may be desired by the applicant. If a patent for a less term than 15 years has been applied for, it may be subsequently extended to the full term by payment of the proper taxes (see *Taxes*). In the case of an invention already patented abroad, the duration of the Portuguese patent is limited to the unexpired residue of the first foreign patent (see also *Conditions of Grant*).

**Date of Patent.**—The patent is dated as of the day of the signature of the Royal Letters by the King.

**Extent of Grant.**—The patent extends to the whole of Portugal and its Colonies.

**Procedure.**—Duplicate copies of a description of the invention in the Portuguese language must be furnished, accompanied by two sets of drawings on any suitable material, drawn to a metrical scale and of convenient dimensions, legalised power of attorney, etc. The Royal Letters (Alvara) is transmitted to the Ministry of Public Works, Commerce and Industry, signed by the King and the Minister, etc., and issued.

**Official Examination.**—No examination is made as to the novelty or utility of the invention.

**Certificates of Addition.**—Improvements on an existing patent may be protected either by a new patent, or by a certificate of addition to the original patent. A certificate of addition, which enures for the full term of the original patent, can be obtained during the first year after the date of the patent, only by the original patentee or his legal representative, but any one is at liberty to make application for a certificate of addition, even during this period, the application remaining under seal, and having the preference against any other party who may present an application subsequently. In any case, however, the original patentee has the prior claim if he should make application for a certificate of addition at any time during the first year of his patent.

**Conditions of Grant ; working.**—The invention must be worked in Portugal within two years from the date of the signature of the patent, and must not cease to be so worked for two years consecutively. It is not absolutely necessary to have an official certificate of working, but this is desirable as proof in case of subsequent litigation. If the patentee can justify his inaction, the Government may accord a further delay of two years for working, on due application being made.

**Importation and Marking of patented articles.**— The importation by the patentee of articles made in accordance with the patent is not prohibited. The law imposes no obligation on the patentee to mark the patented articles as such.

**Revocation of Patent.**—Patents may be annulled :— (a) if the invention was already made public prior to the date of application for Portugese patent ; (b) if it has already been patented in Portugal ; (c) if it is contrary to law or to public safety or health ; (d) if the title given fraudulently includes a different object ; (e) if the description fails to specify all that is necessary to carry out the invention or the true means employed ; (f) if the proper formalities have not been observed in obtaining the patent ; (g) if the invention is not useful ; (h) if the invention is not put into operation in Portugal within two years from the date of the signature of the patent.

**Assignments.**—The assignment wholly or in part must be under certificate of a notary. There is no provision for the registration of transfers.

**Infringements.**—The manufacture, sale, or introduction of articles made in accordance with the invention, into Portugal or the colonies, are considered infringements of the patent. Infringers may be punished by fine, and by the confiscation of all objects used in the production of the patented article besides being liable for damages.

# Russia.

——o——

The population of Russia is about 86,000,000. Considerable progress has been recently made in the manufacture of leather, both ordinary and morocco. Among other manufactures may be mentioned cotton twist and cotton goods, woollen and linen goods, silks, cashmere shawls, carpets, oil, wax, glue, and tobacco.

The silver rouble of 100 copecks is nominally equal to about 3s. 2d., but varies according to the rate of exchange. Paper money is in general use. The pound is equal to 0·902 avoir., the pood (40 lbs. Russian) is equal to 36 lbs. avoir.

---

*(The laws regulating the grant of letters patent are dated 17th June, 1812, the 22nd November, 1833, the 23rd October, 1840, the 15th August, 1845, the 7th July, 1852, the 22nd May, 1862, the 16th February, 1867, the 22nd April, 1868, and the 30th March, 1870.)*

Letters patent can be obtained for inventions already patented abroad and also for inventions which are already known and in use in foreign countries, but are new in Russia, and for which no foreign patent has been granted. The former are termed Patents of Invention ; the latter, which are termed Patents of Importation, can only be obtained by special favor, the advantages to be derived from the introduction of the inventions being taken into consideration.

**To whom granted.**—Patents are granted to the inventor or his assignee, and to the introducer of foreign inventions known abroad, but which are new in Russia.

**For what granted.**—Patents of Invention are granted, for any new and useful art, machine, manufacture, or composition of matter (and any improvement therein) not publicly known in the Empire. Patents of Importation are granted exceptionally and by special favor for the introduction of inventions already known and in use abroad, but which are new in Russia, and for which no foreign patent has been obtained. Patents are not granted for fundamental or elementary principles, unless applied or embodied to obtain some new result in the arts, nor for trifling inventions indicative only of inventive genius, and possessing no practical utility or advantage; nor for inventions dangerous to society or detrimental to the government revenues. No patents are granted for inventions relating to purposes of war and national defence, such as guns, projectiles, fuses, and other ordnance appurtenances, armour plating for ships, torpedoes powder magazines, revolving turrets, &c., the use of which appertains to Government alone. Patents are, however, granted for improvements in small arms, cartridges, and other like inventions, which are applicable both for military and private use, but only on the condition that the army and navy shall not be thereby debarred from the free use of such inventions for military purposes.

**Novelty of Invention.**—An invention is considered new and a Patent of Invention may be obtained therefor, if the invention is not already in use in the Empire, and if no detailed description has, prior to the application for the patent, been published in the Empire.

**Duration of Patent.**—Patents of Invention are granted for three, five, or ten years, at the option of the applicant, but the patent, when once granted for either of the short terms, cannot be subsequently prolonged. The duration of the grant is in any case limited to the duration of a previous foreign patent (if any) for the same invention. Patents of Importation are granted for terms varying from one to six years.

**Date of Patent.**—The term of the patent is computed from the day of issue of the grant.

**Extent of Grant.**—The patent extends to the Empire of Russia and the Kingdom of Poland.

**Procedure.**—A petition, together with a full and clear specification in the Russian language, containing a distinct statement of what is claimed, accompanied by drawings illustrating the invention, is presented to the Minister of the Interior, and thereupon a certificate is issued setting forth the date and hour at which the application was presented. Priority is acquired from the time of filing, and actions for infringement can be at once instituted. The application is then submitted to the Committee of Manufactures for examination, and a report is made to the Minister of Finance, stating whether the invention has or has not been previously patented in Russia. If the description is considered incomplete, the applicant is required to amend the same. The patent is not, however, under ordinary circumstances issued until after the lapse of about 18 months from the date of application. The issue of the grant is advertised in the newspapers.

**Model.**—If the invention relates to firearms, surgical instruments, or artificial building materials, a model or specimen must be supplied; also when necessary for the comprehension of the invention.

**Official Examination.**—The application is submitted to an examination as regards the novelty, and also as to the merit of the invention, by the Committee of Manufactures. The grant of the patent, while it affords no proof that the applicant is the true and first inventor, certifies that the invention has not been previously patented in Russia.

**Taxes.**—The patent is subject only to the fees on application, the amount of which depends upon the term of years applied for. There are no subsequent taxes payable to maintain the patent in force.

**Conditions of Grant ; working.**—The invention must be put into operation in the Empire within one quarter of the term for which application for the patent is made, and this period is computed from the day on which the petition is presented. A certificate of working must be obtained and filed at the Ministry.

**Importation and Marking of patented articles.—** The law does not prohibit the importation of the patented articles by the patentee, and imposes no obligation to mark the patented articles as such.

**Revocation of Patent.—**The patent may be revoked upon failure to present within the prescribed time to the proper department a certificate that the invention has been worked, or upon proof that the invention had been introduced or completely published in the Empire prior to the application ; or that a Patent of Invention had been obtained under circumstances when only a Patent of Importation could be legally granted ; or that the patent was fraudulently obtained ; or that the specification is insufficient.

**Assignments.—**All assignments, &c., must be recorded, and certain legal formalities fulfilled. Patentees may not transfer their rights to joint stock companies, without the special permission of the Government.

# Finland.

——o——

The Grand Principality of Finland has a population of about 200,000, and the capital is Helsingfors. It has a semi-independent form of government. It has nominally preserved its ancient constitution with a national parliament of four estates, but is really governed by a Governor General and Senate appointed by the Emperor of Russia.

*(Patent Law of* 1876.)

Letters Patent for the Grand Principality of Finland are granted by the Governor-General.

**To whom granted.**—Patents are granted to the true inventor.

**For what granted.**—Patents are granted for new and useful inventions and improvements in the arts and manufactures. Patents are not granted for medicines nor for inventions the use of which would be contrary to public morality or safety.

**Novelty of Invention.**—The invention must not have been completely published in Finland, nor introduced into use there. In the case of inventions made elsewhere and already patented in another country, the publication of the specification of the foreign patent will not invalidate the Finnish patent.

**Duration of Patent.**—Patents are granted for terms varying from three to 12 years, at the option of the Government. In fixing the term for which the patent shall be granted, regard is had to the condition of that branch of industry in Finland to which the invention relates, or to which it is most nearly allied. The term for which the patent is originally granted cannot be extended. In the case of inventions already patented in another country, the duration of the Finnish patent is limited to that of the previous foreign patent for the same invention. The duration of the patent is in all cases subject to the condition hereafter mentioned as to working the invention (see *Conditions of Grant*).

**Date of Patent.**—The patent dates from the day of issue.

**Extent of Grant.**—The patent extends to the Grand Principality of Finland.

**Procedure.**—The application must contain a full and complete specification, describing the invention and the means of carrying the same into effect, and distinguishing clearly the particular features of novelty which constitute the invention or improvement and accompanied by drawings and models (if required), and a certified copy of the previous foreign patent (if any), stating its date and the term for which it was granted. This specification must be published, at the patentee's expense, in two Finnish newspapers in the Finnish and Swedish languages.

**Official Examination.**—An official examination is made as to the novelty and utility of the invention before the patent is granted.

**Taxes.**—The patent is subject to a tax of twenty Finnish marks for each year of the term for which the patent is granted, which must be paid up in full. In addition to these taxes there are sundry petty expenses connected with the registration of the application and the issue of the patent.

**Conditions of Grant; working invention.**—The patentee is required, at his own expense, to publish the specification of his invention *in extenso* in two Finnish newspapers in the Finnish and Swedish languages, within two months from the date of issue of the patent. The patentee is generally required to bring the invention into practical operation in Finland within two years. In some cases one year only is allowed, and in others the term may, on special application, be prolonged to four years.

In any case the patentee must subsequently furnish proof every year that the invention continues to be so worked in the principality.

**Revocation of Patent.**– The patent will be cancelled if the patentee fails to publish his invention as above mentioned, or to work it in Finland and furnish proof thereof within the required time (see *Conditions of Grant*); or if it be proved that the invention is of an unpatentable character, or that it was, previous to the application for a patent in Finland, already in use either in Finland or in any other country, or had been already patented.

# Norway.

Norway has few important manufactures. The timber and ship building trades are the most important. There are numerous distilleries, and the iron foundries, machine works, tobacco and lucifer match factories may be mentioned. The trade is chiefly carried on with Great Britain and Germany. Norway comprises an area of about 123,000 square miles, with a population of nearly 2,000,000. The monetary system is the same as that of Denmark. The system of weights and measures used in France has been introduced. The following are also used : Pund = 1.1 lb avoir. Fod = 12.02 English inch. Kande = 3.3 imperial pint. Mill = 7.01 English miles.

*(Law of 1839, and Royal Resolutions of 1841, 1856, 1873, and 1876.)*

The only legal enactment relating to the granting of patents in Norway is contained in § 82 of the law relating to Handicrafts. Patents are granted by the King. By Royal Resolution of the 26th August, 1876, a Committee was appointed to examine into the existing patent regulations, and if necessary to draw up a new law on the subject. The report of this Committee has not however yet been published.

**To whom granted.**—Patents are granted to any person, whether the inventor or importer.

**For what granted.**—Patents are granted for new inventions in arts and manufactures.

**Novelty of Invention.**—The invention must be new, that is to say it must not have been published or practised in Norway prior to the application for a patent.

**Duration of Patent.**—The maximum term for which the patent can granted is 10 years, subject to the conditions as to working the invention hereafter mentioned (see *Conditions of Grant*).

**Date of Patent.**—The patent dates and runs from the date of issue, which may be from three months to one year subsequent to the date of application.

**Extent of Grant.**—The patent extends to the Kingdom of Norway.

**Procedure.**—The application is made by a petition addressed to the Department of the Interior, and must be accompanied by the prescribed fee and a full and complete specification in the Norwegian language, together with drawings in duplicate, in all cases where the nature of the invention requires them. The application is first referred to experts, and then submitted to His Majesty's decision. In case of refusal the official fee is repayable.

**Official Examination.**—A strict examination is made as to the novelty and utility of the invention.

**Taxes.**—The patent is not subject to the payment of any taxes after the issue of the grant.

**Conditions of Grant; working invention.**—The patent is usually granted subject to the condition that it shall become void if the invention be not brought into practical use in Norway within two years.

**Importation and Marking of patented articles.**—The law does not prohibit the importation by the patentee of articles made in accordance with the patent, and does not require patented articles to be marked as such.

**Revocation of Patent.**—The patent is liable to annulment upon proof that the invention was destitute of novelty when the patent was applied for, and becomes void by neglect to work the invention as prescribed (see *Conditions of Grant*).

**Assignments.**—The law does not require assignments to be registered, but it is usual to do so.

# Sweden.

———o———

The manufactures of Sweden are principally carried on in Stockholm (the capital), Gothenburg, and Norrköping. In addition to metallurgy, the following may be mentioned, viz., machine making, spinning and weaving cotton and wool, paper making, lucifer matches, leather, glass, and porcelain. There are also tobacco manufactories, sugar refineries, and beetroot sugar manufactories. The population is about 4,600,000.

The monetary system is the same as in Norway and Denmark. The French system of weights and measures is to come into force in 1889. The following are now used, viz. :—

| | |
|---|---|
| Skålpund | = ·937 lb. avoir. |
| Fot | = 11·7 English inches. |
| Kanna | = 4·6 Imperial pints. |
| Mil | = 6·64 English miles. |

---

*(Royal Ordinance dated August 19th, 1856, as amended by Decree of February 22nd, 1867.)*

Patents are granted for the exclusive right of working and using new inventions and improvements in manufactures and arts for a limited term, to be fixed by the Chamber of Commerce.

**To whom granted.**—Patents are granted to the actual inventor, whether a native or foreigner.

**For what granted.**—Patents are granted for new inventions concerning objects of art and industry; for improvements in old inventions already patented, provided such improvements are not covered by patents previously granted, but not for medicines or inventions contrary to law, public safety or morality, nor for abstract principles, but only for their application to an invention, the working or method of which must be clearly described in the application.

**Novelty of Invention.**—The invention must be new in Sweden. In the case of inventions already patented abroad, the publication of the specification of the foreign patent does not prevent a patent being obtained in Sweden.

**Duration of Patent.**—Patents are granted for not less than three years or more than 15 years, the term depending on the nature and importance of the invention, but in the case of an invention already patented abroad, the term of the Swedish patent cannot extend beyond the term for which the foreign patent has been obtained.

**Date of Patent.**—The patent dates and runs from the date on which the grant is advertised by placard in the hall of the Chamber of Commerce.

**Extent of Grant.**—The patent extends to the Kingdom of Sweden.

**Procedure.**—The application is made by a petition to the Royal Chamber of Commerce, stating the term for which the patent is demanded and containing a full description of the invention with drawings, and accompanied by a declaration. The application is examined by the Chamber of Commerce, which fixes the time for which the patent is granted. The patent is then issued and published by placards in the hall of the Chamber of Commerce.

**Official Examination.**—A formal examination is made as to the clearness and sufficiency of the specification, but none as to the novelty or utility of the invention.

**Taxes.**—The patent is not subject to any taxes after the first application.

**Conditions of Grant ; working invention.** — The whole patent and specification must be published three times in the official newspaper at the applicant's expense, within three months from the day on which the patent was advertised.

The invention must be brought into full practical operation within the Kingdom within two years from the issue of the patent, and proof thereof must be furnished to the Chamber of

Commerce. This period may, upon good cause being shown, be extended to four years at most, according to circumstances. The patentee must, moreover, furnish proof annually throughout the duration of the patent that the invention continues to be worked within the Kingdom.

**Revocation of Patent.**—Patents become null and void by breach of the conditions as to working the invention, and are liable to be declared void upon proof that the invention has been previously patented or worked in Sweden by any other party, or that the specification is insufficient, or that the patentee is not the original inventor, or that the invention is not susceptible of being patented.

**Assignments.**—Assignments and licenses must be registered at the Chamber of Commerce.

**Infringements.**—Infringements are punishable by a fine of from 100 to 200 kroner for a first offence, and from 200 to 400 kroner for a second offence (half of which goes to the patentee), besides damages.

# Denmark.

——o——

The manufactures of Denmark are comparatively insignificant. There are iron foundries, sugar refineries, tanneries, and distilleries. The manufacture of paper is extensive.

The colonial possessions of Denmark (to which the Danish patent may on application be extended) are Iceland, the Faroe Islands, and the West Indian Islands of St. Thomas, Santa Cruz, and St. Juan, which chiefly produce sugar.

The area of Denmark, including the Faroe Islands, is upwards of 15,000 square miles with a population of upwards of 2,000,000.

The unit of the monetary system is the krona or crown $= 1/1\frac{1}{3}$ ; 18 kroner $= £1$. The krona is divided into 100 öre.  100 lbs. Danish $= 110\frac{1}{4}$ lbs. avoir.

Inventions are protected by Royal Letters Patent, granted through the Minister of the Interior, in accordance with rules prescribed by the traditional practice of that department.

**To whom granted.**—Patents are granted to any person whether the inventor or merely the importer.

**For what granted.**—Patents are granted for all inventions which are novel in principle or practice, but not for medicines.

**Novelty of Invention.**—The invention must be new, that is to say, it must not have been published in a printed work, nor used in Denmark prior to the application for the patent.

**Duration of Patent**—Patents are usually granted for five years.  In rare cases the term may be ten or even 15 years, but five years is the term for which patents are granted to foreigners.  The duration of the patent is subject, however, to the condition hereafter mentioned as to working the invention (see *Conditions of Grant*).

**Date of Patent.**—The patent dates and runs from the date of issue, which may be from three months to one year subsequent to the date of application.

G

**Extent of Grant.**—Patents ordinarily extend to the Kingdom of Denmark only, but on special applications made, they may be extended so as to include the Danish possessions of Iceland, the Faroe Islands, and the West Indian islands of St. Thomas, Santa Cruz, and St. Juan, a special application being required for each.

**Procedure.**—The application is made by a petition, accompanied by a full and complete specification in the Danish language, together with drawings in duplicate. The documents are filed at the Ministry of the Interior, and are forwarded thence to the technical advisers of the Crown, by whom a report is made, stating whether the invention is new and deserving of protection, and if so, for what term. The patent is then issued or refused, according the nature of this report.

**Official Examination.**—An examination is made as to the novelty and utility of the invention.

**Taxes.**—The patent is not subject to the payment of any taxes after the issue of the grant.

**Conditions of Grant; working invention.**—The invention must be worked in Denmark within one year of the date of the patent, and must continue to be so worked throughout the term of the patent.

**Importation and Marking of patented articles.**—The law does not prohibit the importation into Denmark of articles made in accordance with the patent, whether such importation be carried on by the patentee or by any other person without his license or consent.

**Revocation of Patent.**—The patent is liable to annulment upon proof that the invention was destitute of novelty at the time of making application, or that the patentee has failed to work the invention as prescribed (see *Conditions of Grant*).

**Assignments.**—The law does not require assignments and licenses to be registered, but it is usual to do so.

# Luxembourg.

————o————

The Grand-Duchy of Luxembourg lies between Prussia, France and Belgium,
and has an area of 999 square miles. Iron ore is obtained in considerable quantity. French is the official language. The population is about 206,000. The
King of the Netherlands is the Grand Duke.

The system of money, weights and measures is the same as that of France.
The town of Luxembourg is the capital.

---

(*Patent Law of June 30th, 1880.*)

Letters Patent for the Grand-Duchy of Luxembourg are
granted by the King of the Netherlands, Prince of Orange-
Nassau, Grand-Duke of Luxembourg, &c. Certificates of
Addition for improvements on inventions which are already
patented in the Grand-Duchy are also granted.

**To whom granted.**—Patents are granted to the first
inventor, his heirs and assigns.

**For what granted.**—Patents are granted for new inventions capable of being practically applied in industry, but not
for inventions contrary to the laws or to morality, nor for
articles of food or beverages, nor for pharmaceutical products or
substances obtained by chemical means, except it be for a
specific process for the manufacture of the said articles or substances.

**Novelty of Invention.**—The invention must not, prior
to the date of application, have been so clearly described in
printed publications, or be so notoriously used, either in the
Grand-Duchy or in one of the States of the German Commercial
League, as to enable others skilled in the art to put it in
practice.

G 2

**Duration of Patent.**—The duration of the patent is 15 years, subject to the conditions as to working (see *Conditions of Grant*), and the payment of taxes (see *Taxes*), and to the condition that a patent for the same invention be applied for within three months, and duly obtained, in the States with which the Grand-Duchy is associated by a commercial league, and to the further condition that the life of the patent in the Grand-Duchy is dependent on that of such foreign patent or patents. The expiration by non-working of such foreign patent does not however, entail the lapsing of the Luxembourg patent.

**Date of Patent**—The patent dates and runs from the day after application.

**Extent of Grant.**—The patent extends to the Grand-Duchy of Luxembourg.

**Procedure.**—The application is made by a declaration, accompanied by a specification in French or German, together with drawings on a metrical scale, models or specimens (all in duplicate), a power of attorney and a receipt for the first year's tax. In case of rejection an appeal lies to the Council of State. In case of contention the first applicant is entitled to the patent, provided he be the inventor.

If the application be made by a foreigner, he must elect a domicile in the Grand-Duchy, and appoint a representative, to whom all communications will be made.

**Official Examination.**—Thepatent is granted without preliminary examination as to the novelty or utility of the invention.

**Taxes.**—The patent is subject to the payment of an annual and progressive tax, commencing at 10 francs, and increasing 10 francs per annum. Three months' grace is allowed for these payments. Certificates of Addition are exempt from all taxes after the first year.

**Certificates of Addition.**—Certificates of Addition are granted for improvements in an invention which is already patented. They are annexed to, and expire with, the original patent, and are exempt from annual taxes. Certificates of Addition obtained by one of the co-owners of a patent are available by all. The patentee may obtain an original patent for improvements on his own invention in lieu of a Certificate of Addition if he prefers.

**Conditions of Grant ; working.**—The patent is subject to the condition that the invention be brought into practical operation in the Grand-Duchy to a suitable extent within three years of the date of the patent, or at least that the necessary steps be taken to ensure the working of the invention.

**Importation and Marking of patented articles.**—The law does not prohibit the importation by the patentee of articles made in accordance with the patent, nor require patented articles to be marked as such, A penalty is provided for falsely marking or advertising, &c., articles as patented when no valid patent has been obtained.

**Revocation.**—The patent lapses by efflux of time; by non-payment of the annual taxes within the prescribed period; by failure to apply for a patent for the same invention in the States with which the Grand-Duchy is associated by a commercial league, within three months of the date of the patent in the Grand-Duchy, or if upon due application made, such other patent be either refused, or be granted and afterwards revoked, annulled, or otherwise caused to expire, except upon the ground of non-working. The Luxembourg patent is also liable to be revoked upon the ground of non-working (see *Conditions of Grant*); or that the invention is not patentable; or that it has been obtained from a third party without his consent; or that the application is false and fraudulent, or the specification insufficient. An action for nullity may be instituted by any person having an interest therein.

**Compulsory Licenses.**—After three years from the date of the patent it may be declared by Royal Grand-Ducal decree, upon the advice of the Council of State, that the public interest requires that the right of working the invention shall be conceded also to one or more other persons who have applied therefor.

In such case the terms as regards payment, &c., to be made to the patentee will, in the event of disagreement, be settled judicially. By a similar decree the patent may be thrown open, in which case the patentee would be entitled to an indemnity from the State.

**Infringements.**—The penalty for knowingly infringing is a fine of from 100 francs to 2000 francs, besides damages, and in the case of a second offence, imprisonment.

The Court may order the destruction or confiscation of the counterfeit articles, and the apparatus which have been, or are intended to be, used in producing them. The Patent does not avail against any person who, at the time the application was made, had already brought the invention into operation in the Grand-Duchy, or taken the necessary steps to do so.

# Turkey.

———o———

There are scarcely any large m nufactories except in Constantinople, and even there they are few. The cu'tivation of tobacco is very general, and in some parts a considerable source of wealth. Accounts are generally kept in grush or piastres, the value of which is about 2¼d. sterling. 100 piastres make a Turkish lira or gold mejidié (a little more than 18s.), and 500 make a "purse." The unit of weight is the oke=2 5-6th lbs. avoir., and it is divided into 400 drem. The cantar (44 okes) is used for large weights. Liquids are sold by weight; the principal dry measure is the kilo, which varies in different districts. At Constantinople 100 kilos =12¾ imperial quarters. The usual linear measure is the arshin, which is equal to 28 inches.

———————

## (*Patent Law of March 2nd*, 1880.)

The law provides for the granting of Patents of Invention, Patents of Improvement and Certificates of Addition.

**To whom granted.**—Patents are granted to the author or inventor, whether native or foreigner. The author of an invention, already patented in another country, is likewise entitled to obtain a patent in Turkey.

**For what granted.**—Patents are granted for new industrial products and new means, or the new application of known means of obtaining an industrial product or result, but not for pharmaceutical compounds and medicines of all kinds. The application must be limited to a single main subject, and its details.

**Novelty of Invention.**—The invention must not, prior to the date of application in Turkey, have received sufficient publicity either in Turkey or elsewhere, to have been put into actual use.

**Duration of Patent.**—The maximum duration is 15 years from the date of application, subject to the payment of an annual tax (see *Taxes*), and to the condition, in the case of an invention already patented elsewhere, that the Turkish patent will expire with that previously obtained in the foreign country, subject also to the conditions hereafter mentioned as to working and importing the invention (see *Conditions of Grant*).

**Date of Patent.**—Patents bear date as of the day of filing the application.

**Extent of Grant.**—The patent extends to the whole of the Ottoman Empire.

**Procedure.**—The application must consist of a description of the invention (in the Turkish language) and drawings (in duplicate) with a power of attorney, a memorandum of the documents, and a receipt for the first year's tax, and must be lodged under seal at the Ministry of Commerce and Agriculture at Constantinople. In the case of inventions of arms, tools, or apparatus of war, which may be used by the army and navy, the inventors and their applications are directed at once to the Grand Master of Artillery, and to the Imperial Admiralty. A patent will be granted for any invention which is shown to be useful and advantageous to the State after examination, and will be bought in conformity with a contract with the inventor and paid for in proportion to its usefulness by that department of the army and navy which it chiefly concerns.

**Official Examination.**—No official examination is made as to the novelty or utility of the invention, except in the case of inventions mentioned in the last paragraph.

**Taxes.**—Patents are subject to the payment of an annual tax of two Turkish pounds.

**Patents of Improvement and Certificates of Addition.**—The inventor or his assignee has during the term of one year from the date of the original patent, the exclusive right of obtaining a Patent of Improvement for changes or additions to the invention forming the subject of the original patent. But any other person desirous of patenting improvements in an invention already patented by another, may, during the said year, lodge an application under seal. At the expiration of the year, the seal will be broken, and the patent issued. The original patentee will however, have the right of precedence for any Patent of Improvement or Addition, which he may himself have applied for during the said year.

Patents of Addition are granted only to the original patentee or his assignee during the whole duration of the original patent for improvements intimately connected with the subject of the original patent. Such patents are obtained in the same way as original patents, and are annexed to, and expire with, the original patent to which they relate. Patents of Addition are not subject to the payment of any annual taxes.

**Conditions of Grant.**—The invention must be brought into practical operation in Turkey within two years from the date of the patent, and such working must not be subsequently discontinued for two consecutive years unless in either case sufficient reason can be shown for failure to comply with this condition.

**Importation and Marking of patented articles.**— The importation of the patented articles into Turkey is prohibited under penalty of invalidating the patent, but a special permit may be obtained for the introduction of models of machines, and articles intended for public exhibitions or experiments made with the consent of the Government.

Medals will be awarded to the authors of inventions useful to the State, and the design of the medal is to be reproduced by the patentee as a trade mark for the object invented. A penalty of from 2 to 45 Turkish pounds is imposed for falsely advertising articles as patented when no patent has been obtained, or after the patent has expired.

**Revocation of Patent.**—Patents are null and void if the invention was not new at the time of application, or not of a patentable character, or if it relates to theoretical principles,. methods, systems, discoveries and conceptions without indication of their industrial use, or if the title of the invention gives a false or fraudulent indication of its real object, or if the speci--

fication is insufficient, or does not indicate completely and faithfully the true means employed in the invention.

Patents are forfeited by failure to pay the annual tax in due time, or by failure to work the invention within the prescribed time, and to continue such working (unless in either case the patentee can justify his inaction), or by the importation of the patented articles from abroad.

**Assignments.**—A patent may be assigned wholly or in part. An assignment must be made by a notarial act, and has no validity until registered at Constantinople. Assignees benefit by Patents of Addition issued to the original patentee, and conversely.

# Egypt.

There is no patent law in this country.

# Holland.

The patent laws were repealed some fifteen years ago, since when no patents have been granted in Holland.

# Greece.

The population of this kingdom is about 2,500,000, and the area about 34 700 square miles. The manufactures are exceedingly limited. Leather forms an important industry, and ship-building is carried on at various places. The minerals exported are lead, magnesite, and chromate of iron.

The monetary unit is the drachme (=1 franc), divided into 100 lepta. The French metric system of weights and measures was introduced many years ago, but the old system is still adhered to. In the latter the standard lineal measure is the pike=27 inches ; the standard square measure is the stremma, equal to about one third of an English acre ; the standard weight is the oke=2·8lbs. avoir.; 44 okes=1 cantar, or about 124lbs. avoir.

There is no special law in Greece affecting inventions. The practice of the country places all inventors on the same footing as a person seeking a monopoly, and in either case a special act is required to secure the individual in the possession of the rights which he claims. A Bill for the purpose may be introduced into the Chamber by any Deputy and is treated like any other Bill, and if it passes it defines, according to the circumstances of the case, the limits both as to time and place, within which exclusive privileges are accorded to the party on whose behalf the motion is made.

# Switzerland.

In the Swiss Confederation there are as a general rule no special laws for the encouragement and protection of inventors. Consequently the practice of granting patents does not exist. The only exception is to be found in the canton of Tessin where the local government has the power to grant exclusive privileges within its territory.

# Japan.

A patent law was enacted some years ago in Japan, but it has never been brought into operation.

# China.

There is no patent law in China except that of the British colony of Hong-kong, which see.

# Argentine Republic.

———o———

This South American Republic comprises the Provinces of the Rio de la Plata, Buenos Ayres, being the most important. There are no manufactures of any consequence, and the chief productions are wool, hides, cotton, rice, sugar, indigo and tobacco. Wheat and maize are cultivated, and flax, cocoa, cochineal, madder, and chinchona bark, are also produced. The population in 1880 was about 2,500,000 and the Republic contains about 1,180,000 square miles. The capital is Buenos Ayres.

*(Patent Law of 1864.)*

Article 17 of the Constitution confers on the originators of new discoveries or inventions in any branch of industry the exclusive right of working the same for a limited period, these rights being established and defined by the granting of patents as prescribed by the law of 1864, for which purpose a patent office has been established. Patents are issued under the authority of the Government, by the Commissioner of Patents.

Patents of Invention are granted for original inventions and Certificates of Addition are granted for improvements on patented inventions (see *Certificates of Addition*). Caveats may also be entered and are renewable from year to year.

**To whom granted.**—Patents are granted to the inventor or his assignee including the foreign patentee provided he be the inventor or his assignee.

**For what granted.**—Patents are granted for new discoveries or inventions, including all new products of industry, new means, and the new application of known means, for obtaining an industrial product or result. But not for pharmaceutical compositions, financial schemes, abstract theories without application to industrial use, or inventions contrary to law or morality.

The patentees of inventions abroad can obtain the re-issue or confirmation of their patents in the republic. The invention must in all cases be limited to a single chief object with its accessories and applications.

**Novelty of Invention.**—The invention must not, previous to application being made, have received sufficient publicity in works, pamphlets, or periodicals, either in the country or abroad, to enable it to be put into practice.

**Duration of Patent.**—Patents are granted for five, ten, or 15 years, according to the merit of the invention and the wish of the applicant. In the case of inventions previously patented abroad the duration is limited to ten years, and in no case can it exceed the term of the original patent, with which it lapses. The duration of the patent is conditional upon the payment of the annual taxes mentioned below (see *Taxes*), and is subject also to the conditions as to working the invention in the Republic (see *Conditions of Grant*).

**Procedure.**—The application is made by a petition, addressed to the Commissioner of Patents, and duly stamped, accompanied by a specification in Spanish, drawings (all in duplicate), a power of attorney, duly stamped, and a memorandum of the documents, together with the prescribed fee on application, and a model or a sample in the case of a composition. All alterations in the description must be marked and initialed by the applicant.

All documents must be in the form adopted for public documents, with a left hand margin of one third the width of the sheet. If the applicant be the assignee of the inventor, a duly legalized assignment must accompany the application. Drawings must be made on a metrical scale; they should generally be in perspective, and as small and clear as possible (one copy on cloth-mounted drawing paper and one on tracing cloth), and must have a margin on the right of at least one inch.

**Model.**—The model should be in working order, must be durable, neatly made, and as small as possible. If made of wood it must be painted or varnished. The sample of a composition must be sufficient for analysis and for preservation in the office.

The patent may be refused for non-compliance with the provisions of the law, in which case half the fee paid on application is forfeited.

**Official Examination.**—The application is referred to sub-commissioners to examine as to the novelty and patentability of the invention, the Commissioner granting or refusing the patent according to the result of this examination.

In case of refusal an appeal lies within ten days to the Home Minister, by whom, after investigation, the refusal is confirmed or annulled. In the former case the whole sum deposited is forfeited.

A stamp duty of 25 silver or Spanish dollars or piastres is payable on the letters patent if granted, and on the issue of the patent the patentee and an approved surety are bound to accept bills, each drawn on a 12 cents stamp, as collateral security for the payment of the annual taxes when they become due.

**Taxes.**—The Government fees are 80, 200, or 350 piastres (*pesos fuertes*) according to the term of the patent (besides sundry petty stamp duties). The fees on patents for foreign inventions are on the same scale, and are proportionate to the term granted.

These taxes are payable one half at the time of application and the remainder by yearly instalments, the payment of which must be guaranteed by a bond under the hand and seal of the applicant and one surety.

**Certificates of Addition.**—Improvements on patented inventions, may be protected by Certificates of Addition limited to the residue of the original patent, provided it does not exceed 10 years, except when half that period has expired, or when the improvement lessens by half at least, the cost, time, risk or danger of production, in which and other similar cases, the

Commissioner may fix the term for which the certificate may be granted. Such certificates are granted to the original patentee and also to other persons, and are subject to the same formalities except that the original patentee pays only one fourth, and other persons one half, of the fees on an original patent. Certificates of Addition granted to other parties do not confer the right to use the original patent except on payment to the original patentee of a premium to be fixed by the Commissioner ;. or the original patentee may have the option of working the the improvement, jointly with the improver by obtaining a Certificate of Addition on the same terms as the latter.

**Conditions of Grant ; working.**—The invention must be worked by being brought into operation in the the Republic within two years from the date of issue of the patent and the working must not be subsequently interrupted for two consecutive years except by circumstances beyond the patentee's control or by accident duly certified by the office.

**Revocation of Patent.**—Patents are void (*a*) if the invention is not of a patentable character ; (*b*) if obtained under a fraudulent title not corresponding to the invention ; (*c*) if the specification or drawings are incorrect or incomplete ; (*d*) if in the case of a Certificate of Addition it refers to a patent not actually obtained ; (*e*) or if in the case of a foreign invention the foreign patent has expired; (*f*) or if the invention was already in operation in the Republic at the date of the patent; (*g*) if the invention be not put in operation as prescribed (see *Working*).

No special decree is in any case necessary to annul the patent.

**Assignments.**—Assignments can only be made by a notarial act after paying up the taxes in · full for the whole term of the patent. All assignments must be registered at the Patent Office.

**Infringements.**—Infringements are punishable by a fine of from 50 to 500 piastres, or by imprisonment and forfeiture of the counterfeit articles, without prejudice to any indemnity for losses and damages. Selling, exhibiting, or importing the counterfeit articles are subject to the same penalties. In case of a second offence within five years the penalty is doubled.

# Brazil.

———o———

Brazil is the most extensive State of South America. Its chief towns are Rio de Janeiro(the capital), Bahia, and Recife. It has an area of about 3,288,000 square miles, and is divided into 21 provinces. The mineral wealth is considerable, including gold, silver, platinum, iron, and all kinds of precious stones, as well as coal. The chief articles of export are coffee, sugar, india-rubber, raw cotton, hides, tobacco, Paraguay tea, gold and diamonds. The bulk of the exports are sent from Rio de Janeiro, the next ports in importance in this respect being Saô Paulo, Bahia, Pará and Pernambuco, Except for very small transactions, accounts are usually kept in milreis or 1,000 reis (about 2s. 3d.). The French metric system was adopted in 1862, but the old weights and measures are still used to a certain extent. The population at the census of 1872 (omitting Indians) was 10,168,291.

———

*(Patent law of October 14th, 1882.)*

The law guarantees the exclusive use of any invention or discovery by the concession of a Patent of Invention. Certificates of Improvement are also granted for additions to or improvements on the original patent (see *Certificates of Addition*).

**To whom granted.**—In the case of inventions already patented in other countries, the inventor may obtain confirmation of his rights in Brazil, such confirmation conferring the same rights as a patent conceded in the Empire. But the petition for such confirmation must be made in Brazil within seven months from the date of the application for a patent elsewhere, in which case the inventor's right of priority will not be invalidated by the publication of his invention, or its use or employment, or by another petition. Patents granted in joint names can be used freely by the co-patentees.

**For what granted.**—Patents are granted for new industrial products ; new processes or the new application of known processes for obtaining an industrial product or result; the improvement of a patented invention if it facilitates the manufacture of the product or the use of the patented invention, or if it increases its utility. But not for inventions contrary to law or morality, or of a dangerous or noxious character, or which do not afford a practical industrial result.

**Novelty of Invention.**—Except in the case of inventions already patented elsewhere, the invention is considered new, if it has not, prior to the application for a patent, been employed or used either within or without the Empire, or described in any publication (see *To whom granted*).

**Duration of Patent.**—The maximum duration of a Patent of Invention is fifteen years, but limited in the case of inventions previously patented abroad to the life of the foreign patent, and subject to the payment af an annual tax (see *Taxes*) and to the conditions as to working the invention hereafter mentioned (see *Conditions of Grant*).

Certificates of Addition expire with the original patent to which they are annexed, and are exempt from taxes.

**Date of Patent.**—The duration of the patent is computed from the date of the grant.

**Extent of Grant.**—The patent extends to the Empire of Brazil.

**Procedure.**—The application must be limited to one single invention, and is made by a petition accompanied by a specification in the Portuguese language and drawings in triplicate, to be deposited under seal in the department which the Government shall designate.

**Official Examination.**—No official examination is made as to the novelty or utility of the invention, but when the invention appears to be of an unpatentable character, or to relate to alimentary, chemical or pharmaceutical products, a secret examination of the application will be made, upon the result of which will depend whether a patent shall or shall not be granted.

An appeal lies to the Council of State in case of an adverse decision.

**Taxes.**—Patents of Invention are subject to an annual and progressive tax, commencing at twenty dollars for the first year, and increasing at the rate of ten dollars per annum.

**Certificates of Addition.**—During the first year of a patent the inventor (and his legal successors) has the exclusive right to obtain a patent for improvements of his own invention. Other persons may, however, present their petitions during that period so as to establish their rights. Such Certificates of addition are exempt from taxes; they are appended to the original patent and expire with it.

**Conditions of Grant; working invention.**—The invention must be brought into effective use in the Empire within three years from the date of the patent and such use must not subsequently be suspended for more than one year at a time, except from causes beyond the patentee's control, to be judged sufficient by the Government. By use is meant the effective exercise of the invention and the supply of the products in proportion to their employment or consumption.

**Marking patented articles.**—Penalties are provided for fraudulently marking goods as patented, for continuing to exercise an industry as patented after the patent has expired or been annulled, and for advertising patents without designating the special object for which they were obtained.

**Revocation of Patent.**—Patents may be cancelled if it shall be proved (a) that the invention is of an unpatentable character; (b) that the patentee is not the true and first inventor; (c) that the patentee concealed some essential feature of the invention; or (d) that the title falsely indicates the object of the invention. The patent will lapse by neglect to comply with the conditions as to working the invention in Brazil (see *Conditions of Grant*), or by failure to pay the annual taxes (see *Taxes*), and (if the patentee resides abroad) by omission to appoint an accredited agent to represent him before the Government and Courts.

**Assignments.**—No assignment has any effect until it is registered in the Bureau of Agriculture, Commerce, and Public Works.

**Infringements.**—The manufacture of the patented products, or the use of the patented processes, without license, or the importation, sale, exposure for sale, or reception for the purpose of sale, of the counterfeit products, knowing them to be such, are considered infringements, and such infringements are punishable by fine of from $500 to $5,000 to the Government, and from 10% to 50% of the damage caused to the patentee.

# Chili.

—o—

This is a republic in South America. It is divided into 19 provinces, with an area of about 182,790 square miles. The mineral productions are of great importance, consisting of gold, silver, copper, coal, lead, and iron. The exports are metals, flour, hides, wheat, &c. The population in 1882 was 2,234,000.

*(Patent laws of 1840 and 1872.)*

Article 152 of the Chilian Constitution, dated May, 1833, accords to every author or inventor the exclusive right to his discovery or invention for a limited time. This is defined by the law of 1840, which (amended by the law of 1872) now regulates the granting of patents.

**To whom granted.**—Patents are granted to the actual author or inventor.

**For what granted.**—Patents are granted for new inventions or improvements in an art, manufacture, machine, instrument, or preparation of materials. But not for the mere introduction into Chili of foreign arts and industries.

**Novelty of Invention.**—The invention must be original and unknown in the country.

**Duration of Patent.**—The duration of the patent is determined by the President of the Republic, and cannot exceed ten years. The term of the patent is computed from the expiration of the term allotted for working the invention (see *Conditions of Grant*).

The term of the patent may be extended, upon application, made six months before the expiration of the original term, but only when owing to accident or unforseen circumstances, the patentee is judged deserving of it.

**Extent of Grant.**—Patents may be conceded for the whole Republic or for one or more provinces.

**Procedure.**—The application, containing a faithful, clear, and ·succinct description of the invention in the Spanish language, accompanied by a declaration that it is original and unknown in the country, and by samples, drawings, or models must be laid before the Home Minister who refers it to experts on whose report the Minister grants or withholds the patent. The application is advertised and may be opposed. The patent is issued under the signature of the President and the seal of the Republic upon payment of $50 into the Treasury and proof of deposit in the National Museum of the drawings or model of the invention, together with a full and specific description of the invention, distinguishing the new from the old parts, which is signed by the Commissioners and is preserved closed under the private seal of the inventor, until the expiration of the patent. In case of fraud, or of rival applications, or of non-working of the invention, the seal may be broken.

**Official Examination.**—An examination is made by a commission of experts as to the novelty and utility of the invention and its probable effect on industry or commerce, and as to the difficulties and expenses incurred by the applicant, in order to. regulate the terms to be fixed for putting the invention into practice, and for the duration of the patent.

**Taxes.**—The patent is not subject to any taxes beyond those on the first application.

**Conditions of Grant; working invention.**—A proportionate term, exclusive of the period allotted for the patent, is fixed for the establishment of the machinery, &c., for working the invention. The patent begins to run from the expiration of this term. If the invention has not been brought into practical operation within the prescribed term, or if it subsequently ceases to be worked for more than one year at a time, or if the products become inferior to the original sample, the patent is annulled.

**Assignments.**—Patents may be assigned, provided the Home Minister be previously notified thereof, and of the reasons therefor. If the latter are found good the assignment is registered.

**Infringements.**—Infringers are liable to a fine of $100 to $1,000 and to the forfeiture of the counterfeit articles and of the machinery and tools used in their manufacture, the proceeds being divisible between the Treasury and the patentee. Any person not being the true inventor, obtaining a patent under false pretences is liable to a similar fine and to from three to twelve months imprisonment.

# United States of Colombia.

—o—

This is a federal republic comprising the following States:—Antioquia, Bolivar, Boyaca, Cauca, Cundinamarca, Magdalena, Panama, Santander and Tolima, and is situated in the north-western part of South America, and the Isthmus of Panama, having a total area of about 320,000 square miles. The population in 1876 was 3,000,000.

Tobacco, coffee, cocoa, and chinchona bark are the only vegetable exports of any importance. The mineral wealth of the country is considerable, gold and silver mines being the most important. There are no manufactures worth mentioning.

The capital is Bogotá.

---

## (*Patent Law of* 1869.)

Patents of Invention are granted by the National Executive power of the Union for the exclusive right to make use or sell new inventions or discoveries.

**To whom granted.**—Patents are granted to the inventor including the patentee of a foreign invention

**For what granted.**—Patents are granted for any invention or improvement in a machine, mechanical apparatus, combination of materials, method or process, susceptible of useful application to industry, arts, or sciences, and for the making and sale of any manufacture or industrial product; but not for the importation of foreign products or manufactures, nor for inventions which endanger the public health or security. Inventions patented abroad, may also be patented in Colombia, provided they have not been brought into public use in Colombia.

**Novelty of Invention.**—The invention must be new in Colombia.

**Duration of Patent.**—The duration of the patent is from 5 to 20 years, at the option of the applicant, subject to the condition as to working the invention hereafter mentioned (see *Conditions of Grant*), and subject to the condition that the Colombian patent shall expire with the prior foreign patent (if any) for the same invention.

**Date of Patent.**—The patent dates from the day of issue.

**Extent of Grant.**—Patents extend to the whole of the United States of Colombia.

**Procedure.**—Patents are obtained on petition to the executive power, setting forth the nature of the invention, and stating the number of years applied for, and accompanied by a full and complete description of the invention, with drawings and a sample or model if necessary. The executive decree granting the patent is published twice in the *Official Gazette*. Patents may be refused if the provisions of the law have not been complied with, or if the invention encroaches on existing rights.

**Official Examination.**—No examination is made as to the novelty or utility of the invention.

**Taxes.**—The application must be accompanied by a fee of 10 dollars, and if the patent be granted the whole of the fees must be paid up in advance for the full term of the patent, at the rate of from 5 to 10 dollars per annum, the application fee being reckoned as part payment.

**Conditions of Grant; working invention.**—The patent lapses if the invention be not brought into practical operation or use within a whole year, unless the patentee can justify his inaction.

**Revocation of Patent.**—A patent is void when it violates vested rights, and anyone whose rights may have been encroached upon by the patent may appeal to the Courts for its revocation.

**Infringements.**—An injunction may be obtained for the infringement of a patent, the offender being dealt with in conformity with the penal laws of the Union.

# Costa Rica.

——o——

This is the southernmost of the Central American republics, containing an area of about 26,040 square miles, and a population estimated at 200,000.

The commerce is principally with Great Britain, and coffee is by far the largest export. Sugar, maize, cocoa, sarsaparilla &c. are also exported. The Constitution dating from 1871 vests the legislative authority in a Congress of one Chamber, chosen in electoral assemblies, the members of which are returned by universal suffrage. The Executive is in the hands of a President assisted by two vice-presidents.

The capital is San José.

———

Article 20 of the Constitution states that it appertains to Congress to promote the progress of arts and sciences, and to secure for a limited time to inventors the exclusive right of their discoveries. Applications for Patents of Invention must therefore be made to the Constitutional Congress.

# Ecuador.

——o——

This is a republic situate between Colombia and Peru. There are practically no manufactures carried on in Ecuador with the exception of Panama hats and other articles made from palm straw. The chief exports are cocoa, cascarilla, vegetable ivory, caoutchouc, straw hats, coffee, hides &c.; gold, silver, lead, quicksilver, and sulphur, are obtained. The metric system of weights and measures prevails. The population in 1878 was about 1,150.000. The capital is Quito. The chief coin is the peso or piastre about equal to 4s.

———

Patents are granted in this Republic for terms varying from five to 20 years at the option of the applicant, for inventions which have not already been patented elsewhere. Patents for foreign inventions already patented elsewhere expire with the previous foreign patent. No official examination is made as to the novelty or utility of the invention.

# Guatemala.

———0———

This is the northernmost of the republican States of Central America and has an area of 40,776 square miles and a population of 1,500,000.

The most important export is coffee and next in importance, although of considerably less value, are cochineal, hides, and sugar.

The capital is New Guatemala.

## (*Patent Law of* 1864.)

Patents of Invention and Patents of Importation are granted by the President under the seal of the Republic and confer the exclusive proprietorship of new inventions.

**To whom granted.**—Patents are granted to the actual inventor or importer of a new invention.

**For what granted.**—Patents are granted for any new invention in, or improvement of, any art, manufacture, machine, instrument or preparation of material.

**Novelty of Invention.**—The invention must be new in the Republic.

**Duration of Patent.**—The duration of patents for original inventions cannot exceed ten years, and of patents for the introduction of arts, industries or machines which are known in other countries but are new in the Republic, eight years and under, according to their utility, &c. Prolongations may be obtained in very exceptional cases and must be applied for at least six months before the expiration of the original term.

**Date of Patent.**—The date from which the duration of the patent is computed, is the expiration of the term allotted for working the invention. (See *Conditions of Grant.*)

**Extent of Grant.**—The patent may extend either to the whole Republic, or to one, two, or more Departments.

**Procedure.**—The application is made by lodging a petition and affidavit accompanied by a description of the invention in Spanish, together with drawings, and a receipt for the payment of 50 dollars.

**Conditions of Grant; working invention.**—A proportionate time is fixed within which the invention must be brought into practical operation in the Republic, from the expiration of which term the patent dates and runs. If the invention be not worked within the time allotted, or if it cease to be so worked for more than a year at any subsequent time, the patent will be forfeited.

**Revocation of Patent.**—The patent is forfeited by failure to work the invention within the prescribed time, or if the products are adulterated or inferior to the original samples.

**Assignments.**—Assignments must be registered and the reasons for making the same must be given.

**Infringements.**—Infringers and fraudulent patentees are punishable by a fine and imprisonment.

# Hayti.

—o—

The republic of Hayti is the western or French portion of the Island of San Domingo, which after Cuba is the largest of the West India Islands. Coffee is the chief object of cultivation, and the chief exports are coffee, cocoa, mahogany, and logwood. It is the constant scene of revolutions and the finances of the State are consequently in utter disorder. Capital Port-au-Prince.

This Republic has no law or practice on the subject of Patents for Inventions.

# Hawaiian Islands.

—o—

These islands are in the North Pacific Ocean, and form the Kingdom of Hawaii. Total area about 7,628 square miles. Population, about 72,000. The capital is Honolulu. The exports are mainly sugar, coffee, rice, pulse, hides, &c. and the soil is very fertile.

The Minister of the Interior, with the approval of his Majesty the King, may issue a patent to the inventor or improver of any machine, manufacture, or work of art calculated to improve the interests of science, agriculture, or manufactures, and may therein grant to such inventor or improver for any term of years not exceeding ten, that may be specified in such patent, and upon the granting of such patent, the sum of 100 dollars shall be paid by the patentee, to the Minister of the Interior for the use of the royal exchequer.

Every such inventor or improver shall, before receiving a patent, deliver to the Minister of the Interior a full and clear description in writing of his invention or improvement, and of the mode of using the same, or applying it to the purpose for which it is intended, and of the manner and process of making and constructing or compounding the same; and in case of any machine, he shall also furnish, in addition to the written description, accurate drawings and a complete model thereof, and shall also at the same time if a citizen of this kingdom, deposit with the Minister of the Interior the sum of 30 dollars, and if a foreigner the sum of 100 dollars for the use of the royal exchequer.

Any person who shall have invented any new art, machine, or improvement thereof, and shall desire further time to mature the same, may file in the office of the Minister of the Interior a caveat setting forth the design and purpose thereof, its distinguishing characteristics, and praying protection of his right until he shall have matured the same.

# Liberia.

—o—

This is a republic of Western Africa. The chief exports are coffee, sugar, ginger, palm oil, indigo, ivory &c., The chief town is Monrovia.

## (*Law of* 1864.)

**To whom granted.**—Patents are granted to the original and first discoverer of a new invention or to his assignee.

**For what granted.**—Patents are granted for any new and useful improvement of any art, machine, manufacture, process, or composition of matter, or any new and useful application of any known substance or machine or composition of matter or any new and useful application of any known article of manufacture, device, or apparatus, to any art, manufacture, machine, process or composition of matter.

**Novelty of Invention.**—The invention must not have been known by others within the limits of the Republic prior to the application for patent.

**Duration of Patent**—The duration of the patent is fifteen years.

**Procedure.**—The application is made by a specification and drawings, accompanied by an oath that the applicant is the original and first inventor or his legal assignee, and by a certificate to the same effect under the hand of a notary public or the mayor or governor of the city or state in which the applicant resides together with a tax of 25 dollars in the case of a citizen of the Republic, or 50 dollars in the case of a foreigner.

**Conditions of Grant; working invention.**—The invention must be brought into practical operation within the Republic within three years from the date of the patent and any refusal or neglect of the patentee to comply with this condition will be deemed an abandonment of the patent to the public.

**Assignments.**—Patents may be assigned and all such assignments must be registered.

# Mexico.

——o——

This is a federal republic at the south of the United States between the Pacific Ocean and the Gulf of Mexico. It comprises 27 States besides the federal district wherein is situated the capital and the territory of Lower California, the whole having an area of 741,820 square miles. Population 9,686,777. The minerals are of the first importance, the precious metals ranking first. The growing of sugar, coffee, tobacco, &c. has of late years assumed large proportions. Cotton is indigenous to Mexico. Silver is the chief export, after which come copper ores, cochineal, indigo, flour, hides, &c. The capital is the City of Mexico.

The unit of currency is the dollar about equal to 4/-. The weights generally employed are the old ones of Spain.

---

## (*Patent law of* 1832.)

The President of the United States of Mexico is authorised to grant Letters Patent for the exclusive right to use inventions or improvements in any branch of industry in all the States of the Confederation. The authorities of each of the confederated States are also empowered to grant patents limited to their particular States.

**To whom granted.**—Patents are granted to the inventor or improver, whether native or foreigner.

**For what granted.**—Patents are granted for inventions or improvements in any branch of industry.

**Novelty of Invention.**—The invention must be new within the Mexican Republic. Mere importations are not regarded as inventions, although if the General Congress are of opinion that any branch of industry is of great importance, the importer may, under certain circumstances, obtain an exclusive privilege by making application through the Government to the said Congress.

**Duration of Patent.**—Patents for inventions are granted

for ten years, and Patents for improvements for six years from the date of issue of the Patent. The latter correspond to Certificates of Addition in France and other European states. Prolongations may be applied for.

**Date of Patent.**—The Patent dates and runs from the day of issue.

**Extent of Grant.**—The Patent extends to the whole of the United States of Mexico. Patents limited to any one particular State may also be obtained, the Patent being granted by the authorities of the particular State.

**Procedure.**—The applicant must deliver to the Government, or to the Governor of the State or Territory in which is situated the place where the manufacture is to be carried on, a specification, in the Spanish language, particularly describing the invention, accompanied by drawings, all signed by the applicant, together with models, if such are necessary to fully explain the invention, whereupon a certificate is issued. If the application is not made directly to the Government of the State, the local authorities forward the application, with all the documents, to the Governor, who, after making an entry, transmits them to the Minister of the Interior. The application is then advertised three times, and opportunity offered for the entry of oppositions. If no opposition be entered, a Patent is then delivered to the applicant.

If opposition be entered, the Directing Committee of Industry will hear the parties, and call in experts, and bring about an agreement between the parties if possible, whereupon the Committee will draw up an act embodying the agreement; otherwise the committee will send the papers in the case to the Government, with its opinion thereon. If the opposition is founded on the alleged possession of a prior Patent for the same invention, the Government will examine the opposition, and grant or refuse a Patent to the second applicant, without prejudice to the enforcement of the rights of the first patentee before the courts.

**Official Examination.**—No official examination as to the utility of the invention is made.

I

# Nicaragua.

———o———

This is a republic and the largest state of Central America with a seaboard on both the Atlantic and Pacific Oceans, containing an area of 58,170 square miles with a population of about 30C.000. Managua is the capital but the most important town is Leon on the Pacific coast. Next in size is Granada, a town celebrated for the manufacture of gold wire chains.

---

By the resolutions of the Spanish Cortes, which have been declared in force in this Republic, the inventor, improver or introducer of an invention, is entitled, on application to the proper authority describing the invention, to receive a certificate granting the exclusive right to the invention for 10 years in the case of an inventor, seven years in the case of an improver, and five years in the case of an introducer. These terms may be extended by the sovereign power to 15, 10, and 7 years respectively.

The invention must not have been dedicated to the public, and must be brought into practical operation within two years. The Constitution has, however, given Congress arbitrary power to grant rewards and privileges to inventors, and in practice the rules of the decrees cited above are not followed, but application is made to Congress; which concedes or withholds a Patent, as it sees fit.

# Salvador.

————o————

This is the smallest but most thickly populated of all the South American republics. It extends along the Pacific Coast, and contains an area of about 7,335 square miles, with a population of 554,000. The principal products are indigo, coffee, tobacco, sugar and rice. The balsam of Peru is also an important product. There are rich silver mines, and iron ores are also found. The capital is San Salvador.

The Constitution gives power to the Executive to award and concede exclusive privileges to the authors of useful inventions, but the granting of such privileges is not regulated by any special law. In the few cases which have occurred, the Executive in the exercise of its prerogative has followed the practice of other civilized governments.

# Uruguay.

————o————

This is a republic on the east of South America, having an area of about ,000 square miles, and a population of upwards of 450,000. The principal imports are hardware, agricultural implements, timber, woollen goods, and cotton, and the exports hides, horn, hair, tallow, and wool.

*(Patent Law of* 1853, *and decree of* 1876.)

The executive power is authorized to grant Patents of exclusive privilege in respect of inventions, improvements, or importations of inventions, without guaranteeing the utility or novelty of the invention or improvement.

**To whom granted.**—Patents are granted to the inventor improver, or importer.

12 .

**Duration of Patent.**—The duration of Patents of Invention is ten years, Patents of Importation eight years, and Patents of Improvement six years. The duration of the Patent is however, subject to the conditions hereafter mentioned, as to working the invention. (See *Conditions of Grant.*) In case of *force majeure*, or unforeseen circumstances, the Executive Power may, on application made at least six months before the expiration of the original term, grant a prolongation, not exceeding one third of the term of the Patent.

**Novelty of Invention.**—The invention must be new in the Republic.

**Procedure.**—The applicant must present a petition, accompanied by a clear and succinct description of the invention in the Spanish language, together with samples and drawings, or models, according to the nature of the invention, and an affidavit that he is the proprietor thereof. If the application is allowed, the applicant must, within ten days of such allowance, produce a receipt for the sum of one hundred gold dollars, paid into the General Treasury, as a contribution to the National Museum, wherein are deposited the samples, drawings, or models, and the papers relating to the application. The model must be made of durable materials, well finished, and worthy of a place in the National Museum.

**Official Examination.**—No examination is made as to the novelty or utility of the invention, but the executive power makes a formal examination of the documents to ascertain that they comply with the requirements of the law.

**Conditions of Grant ; working invention.**—The Executive Power fixes a time within which the invention must be brought into practical operation in the Republic. The patentee must report in writing to the Minister of Finance when the invention has been established in the Republic, and if this is done within the prescribed time, the Patent will be confirmed. Neglect to comply with this condition will render the Patent liable to revocation, and if, after public notification, the invention is not so worked within one month's grace beyond the term fixed, the Patent will be absolutely cancelled.

**Revocation.**—Any Patent obtained by false representation in respect of an invention that is already in public use in the Republic will be immediately cancelled, and the fraudulent patentee will be condemned in costs and a fine of 100 dollars or imprisonment for six months, The Patent is liable to be revoked by reason of the patentee's neglect to work the invention within the prescribed time (see *Conditions of Grant*), and the revocation will be publicly notified.

**Assignments.**—Written notice of assignments must be given to tne Minister of Finance and the assignment must be entered on the register.

**Infringements.**—If the courts declare that the rights of the patentee have been infringed, the infringer will be liable for damages, and will be fined 500 dollars or imprisoned for three months.

# Venezuela.

———o———

This is a Federal Republic, situate in South America, and comprising several States and Territories and the district of Caracas, the total area being about 439,200 square miles. The population in 1873 was 1.784,000. The chief exports are coffee, cocoa, sugar, cotton, tobacco, indigo, hides, dyewoods, gold, &c. The monetary unit is the venezolano, about equal to 4s., and divided into 100 centavas. The French metrical system of weights and measures has been adopted. The capital is Caracas

*(Patent Law of 1878.)*

The Government grants Patents for Inventions for terms varying from 5 to 15 years at the option of the applicant.

**To whom granted.**—Patents are granted to the inventor, including the patentee of an invention abroad.

**For what granted.**—Patents are granted for new industrial productions, and new methods or the new application of existing methods to obtain a new or improved result, but not for medicines or financial schemes ; nor for inventions contrary to public morality or security. The Patent must be limited to one principal object, with such details of the applications of the invention as may be necessary. A foreign inventor, who has obtained a Patent abroad, may likewise obtain one in Venézuela, but its duration cannot exceed the term for which the foreign Patent has been granted.

**Novelty of Invention.**—The invention is not deemed new if it has been published either in Venezuela or abroad in such manner as to admit of its practical execution.

**Duration of Patent.**—Patents are granted for 5, 10, or 15 years, subject to the conditions hereafter mentioned as to the payment of taxes (see *Taxes*), and as to working the invention (see *Conditions of Grant*), and subject also to the continuance of the prior foreign Patent (if any) for the same invention.

**Date of Patent.**—Patents date and run from the day of a cation.

**Extent of Grant.**—Patents extend to the whole Republic of Venezuela.

**Procedure.**—The application is made by a petition to the Minister of the Interior, stating the term of years for which the Patent is desired, accompanied by a full and complete specification in Spanish, drawings to a metrical scale (all in duplicate), a memorandum of the documents filed, and a Treasury receipt for the first year's tax. There must be no alterations or erasures, and any words struck out must be initialled and noted.

The documents may be signed by the applicant's representative under a power of attorney to be annexed to the application. Any weights and measures mentioned in the specification must be those of the Republic.

**Official Examination.**—A formal examination of the documents is made, but none is made as to the novelty or utility of the invention. In case the application be rejected as informal it may be amended within three months.

**Taxes.**—Patents are subject to an annual tax of four venezolanos (16s.).

**Conditions of Grant; working invention; importation of patented articles.**—The invention must be brought into practical operation in Venezuela within two years from the date of the Patent, and such working must not subsequently be discontinued for two consecutive years, unless, in either case, the patentee can justify his inaction. The importation from abroad of articles manufactured in accordance with the Patent is prohibited.

**Marking patented articles.**—Penalties of from £2 to £20 are provided for falsely marking articles "patented," or after a Patent has expired, or for using the word "patented" without adding the words " without guarantee of the government."

**Revocation of Patent.**—The Patent is void (*a*) if the invention was not new ; (*b*) or not patentable ; (*c*) or relates only to theoretical principles, &c., of which no practical application is specified ; (*d*) or contrary to public order or morality ; (*e*) or if it falsely indicates the object of the invention ; (*f*) or if the specification is insufficient.   The Patent is cancelled (*a*) for non-payment of the annual taxes within the prescribed time (see *Taxes*) ; (*b*) for omission to work the invention (see *Conditions of Grant*) ; and (*c*) for importing articles manufactured in accordance with the Patent from abroad.   Any person interested may apply to the courts to cancel the Patent.

**Assignments.**—Patents may be assigned wholly or in part but only by due form of law and after the payment in full of the annual taxes for the whole term of the Patent.   The assignment must be registered and advertised in the Gazette.

**Infringements.**—Infringements are deemed forgeries, and are punishable by fine of from £5 to £30, besides damages and the confiscation of the counterfeit articles and of the plant &c., used in their manufacture, to the benefit of the patentee.   The sale or exposure for sale, concealment or introduction into Venezuela of counterfeit articles are deemed infringements and are subject to the same penalty, which is to be doubled for a second offence.

# ANALYTICAL SUMMARIES

## OF THE

# PATENT LAWS OF THE BRITISH COLONIES.

# Australia.

——o——

Australia comprises the provinces of Victoria, New South Wales, South Australia, Queensland, and Western Australia, the collective area being about 3,000,000 square miles. In addition to these there are the colonies of Tasmania and New Zealand. Separate Patents are granted in each of the above colonies.

The useful and precious metals exist in considerable quantities in each of these colonies. In New South Wales there is abundance of gold, copper, iron (mostly hœmatite), coal, lead, silver and tin. The copper mines of South Australia are exceedingly valuable. Queensland ranks next for copper, and in the production of tin surpasses the others; gold, iron and coal are also found in considerable quantities. There are lead, silver and copper mines in Western Australia, and considerable ironstone.

Victoria is the principal gold producing colony. Tin and antimony are also found in Victoria. Wool is the staple product of Australia. The total value of imports for 1880 for the provinces of Victoria, New South Wales. South Australia, and Western Australia was upwards of £45,000,000; and exports about £49,000,000.

# Victoria.

## (*The Patents Statute* 1865.)

Patents are granted for 14 years for the sole working or making of any manner of new manufactures within Victoria and its dependencies.

**To whom granted.**—Patents are granted to the true and first inventor within the colony.

**For what granted.**—Patents are granted for the sole working or making of any manner of new manufacture within Victoria and its dependencies.

**Novelty of Invention.**—The invention is considered new if it has not been published or made known in Victoria.

**Duration of Patent.**—The duration of the Patent is 14 years from its date, subject to the payment of the taxes hereafter mentioned (see *Taxes*), and to the limitation (in the case of foreign inventions for which Letters Patent have been obtained elsewhere prior to the grant of the Victorian Patent) to the duration of the prior foreign Patent which shall first expire. If the foreign Patent has already expired prior to the grant of the colonial Patent, the latter is invalid. Provision is also made for the extension of a Patent in certain cases beyond the term first granted, the application for extension being referred to Commissioners appointed to enquire into the matter.

**Date of Patent.**—The Patent dates from the day of filing the application

**Extent of Grant.**—The Patent extends to the colony of Victoria and its dependencies.

**Procedure.**—The application must be limited to a single invention and is made by depositing with the Chief Secretary a complete specification clearly describing the invention and terminating with a distinct claim, and accompanied by drawings, if necessary, together with a copy or copies thereof. Protection conferring the same rights and privileges as Letters Patent is thereupon granted for six months, during which term the invention may be used and published without prejudice to the Patent to be subsequently granted. The Patent is completed by giving notice to proceed. at which stage the application is advertised in the Govenment Gazette and other colonial newspapers, and opportunity afforded for the entry of oppositions. The Law Officer may call such scientific or other aid as he may deem fit and after considering the application' and hearing objections to the grant (if any) he may issue his warrant for the Letters Patent, which are thereupon prepared and are sealed by the Governor with the seal of the colony. The Law Officer may allow or require the specification to be amended or a new one substituted before the patent issues.

**Official Examination.**—No official examination is made as to the novelty or utility of the invention.

**Taxes.**—The patent is subject to a tax, of £15 payable prior to the expiration of the third year, and to a further tax of £20 prior to the expiration of the seventh year, from the date of the patent. The Letters Patent must be returned in order that these payments may be endorsed thereon.

**Conditions of Grant ; working invention.**—The law imposes no obligation on the patentee to put the invention into practice in the colony, but in order to keep the Patent in force certain taxes are payable. (See *Taxes*).

**Importation and Marking of patented articles.**—The importation by the patentee of the patented articles is not prohibited, and the patentee is under no obligation to mark the patented articles in any way. There are certain penalties for the unauthorised user of the word " Patent," &c.

**Revocation of Patent.**—Letters Patent may be repealed by writ of *scire facias*.

**Amendments and Disclaimers.**—Errors or defects in the specification or title may be subsequently amended, and disclaimers may be entered, by the patentee or assignee, not being such alteration or disclaimer as would have the effect of extending the scope of the grant.

**Assignments and Licences.**—All assignments, licences &c. must be recorded, and in the absence of the proper entry the grantee is deemed the exclusive proprietor of the Patent. Assignments may be in any suitable form and as ordinarily prepared for Great Britain will answer every purpose

# New South Wales.

---o---

The chief product is wool ; and gold, silver, coal, tin, iron, copper, antimony, cotton, wine and tobacco are also produced. The population in 1882 was estimated at about 782,000. The capital is Sydney.

---

*(Letters of Registration Act of 1852.)*

The Governor General is empowered to grant Letters of Registration for inventions under his sign manual and the seal of the colony, having the same effect as Letters Patent in England so far as regards the colony.

**To whom granted.**—Letters of Registration are granted to the inventor, or his agent or assignee.

**For what granted.**—Letters of Registration are granted for any invention or improvement in the arts or manufactures.

**Duration of Privilege.**—The duration of the Letters of Registration is not less than seven and may not exceed 14 years.

**Date of Grant.**—The Letters of Registration date from the day of issue thereof.

**Extent of Grant.**—The privilege extends to the colony of New South Wales and its dependencies.

**Procedure.**—The applicant must petition the Governor and file the proper documents, whereupon the matter is referred to experts who are allowed a certain remuneration. If their report is favorable the Letters of Registration issue and must then be registered in the proper office of the Supreme Court. If the report is unfavorable, an appeal can be made.

**Official Examination.**—A more or less complete examination is made as to the novelty of the invention.

**Taxes.**—The grant is not subject to any payment after the first application.

**Conditions of Grant; working invention.**—The law imposes no obligation to put the invention into practice in the colony.

**Importing and Marking patented articles.**—The importation of the patented articles by the patentee is not prohibited, and the patentee is under no obligation to mark the patented articles in any way.

**Revocation of Grant.**—The grant may be repealed by writ of *scire facias* for the same causes and in the same manner as other grants of the Crown are liable to be repealed.

**Assignments and Licences.**—Assignments and licences must be registered within three days of their execution, so that in case of contracts entered into out of the colony, the documents must be sent out unexecuted, and an agent in the colony authorised by power of attorney to execute them. Assignments may be in any suitable form, and as ordinarily prepared for Great Britain will answer every purpose.

# Queensland,

———o———

The population in 1881 was estimated at about 214,000. The staple product is wool; and sugar, both raw and refined is largely exported. Gold, tin, lead, copper, quicksilver, and antimony are found in large quantities. There are also coal mines in certain parts. The chief town is Brisbane.

*(Letters of Registration Act of* 1852 *of the Colony of New South Wales, continued in force in the Colony of Queensland by order in Council of the* 6*th November,* 1859.)

The Governor General is empowered to grant Letters of Registration for inventions under his sign manual and the seal of the colony, having the same effect as Letters Patent in England so far as regards the colony.

**To whom granted.**—Letters of Registration are granted to the inventor, his agent or assignee.

**For what granted.**—Letters of Registration are granted for any invention or improvement in the arts or manufactures.

**Duration of Privilege.**—The duration of the Letters of Registration is not less than seven, and may not exceed 14 years.

**Date of Grant.**—The Letters of Registration date from the day of issue thereof.

**Extent of Grant.**—The Letters of Registration extend to the colony of Queensland.

**Procedure.**—The applicant must petition the Governor, and file the proper documents, whereupon the matter is referred to experts, who are allowed a certain remuneration. If their report is favorable, the Letters of Registration issue, and must then be registered in the proper office of the Supreme Court. If the report is unfavorable an appeal, can be made.

K

Provisional protection for two successive periods of six months each may be obtained, but this protection is practically useless except to Australians.

**Official Examination.**— A more or less complete examination is made as to the novelty of the invention.

**Taxes.**—The grant is not subject to any payment, after the first application.

**Conditions of Grant ; working invention.**—The law imposes no obligation to put the invention into practice in the colony.

**Importing and Marking patented articles.**—The importation of the patented articles by the patentee is not prohibited, and the patentee is under no obligation to mark the patented articles in any way.

**Revocation of Grant.**—The grant may be repealed by writ of *scire facias* for the same causes and in the same manner as other grants of the Crown are liable to be repealed.

**Assignments and Licences.**—Assignments and licences must be registered within three days of their execution, so that in case of contracts entered into out of the colony the documents must be sent out unexecuted, and an agent in the colony authorised by power of attorney to execute them. Assignments may be in any suitable form, and as ordinarily prepared for Great Britain will answer every purpose.

# South Australia.

——o——

The population in 1882 was about 290,000. The mineral wealth is considerable, the copper mines of Moonta, Wallaroo, and Burra Burra being famous.
The capital is Adelaide.

*(The Patent Act, 1877, and Patent Act Amendment Act of 1881.)*

The Commissioner of Patents under the Act is empowered to perform all acts and things incidental to the grant, issue, or renewal of patents.

**To whom granted.**—Patents are granted to the true and first inventor, or to his assignee, executor, or administrator.

**For what granted.**—Patents are granted for the sole making, using, exercising and vending of any new and useful art, machine, manufacture or composition of matter, or any new and useful improvement in any art, machine, manufacture or composition of matter.

**Novelty of Invention.**—The invention is considered new if it has not been publicly used or offered for sale in the Province prior to the date of the patent. The mere fact, however, of an inventor having exhibited or tested his invention, either publicly or privately, is not in itself deemed ground for the refusal of a patent, nor will it justify others in using the invention provided that such exhibiting has taken place within six months of filing the application.

**Duration of Patent.**—The duration of the patent is 14 years from date of filing the application subject to the payment of the taxes hereafter mentioned (see *Taxes*), to the conditions as to working the invention in the colony (see *Conditions of Grant*), and to the limitation (in the case of foreign inventions) to the duration of the previous foreign patent for the same invention. If the foreign patent has already expired prior to the grant of the colonial patent, the latter is invalid. Provision is however made for the extension of a patent in certain cases for not more than seven years beyond the term first granted.

**Date of Patent.**—The patent dates from the day of filing the application.

**Extent of grant.**—The patent extends to the province of South Australia.

**Procedure.**—A petition setting forth the name and title of the invention, and an address in Adelaide to which notices in respect of the petition may be sent, is presented to the Commissioner, accompanied by the proper declarations, specifications, drawings, &c., whereupon (except in case of application for a patent by any person to whom the Commissioner shall have already refused to grant a patent for an invention substantially the same as that for which such application is made) the invention is protected for six months. The application is then advertised in the Government Gazette three times, in at least two daily papers in Adelaide, and opportunity afforded for the entry of objections. The matter is referred to an examiner, whose remuneration is determined by the Commissioner, and if his report is favorable the patent is sealed and issued in due course. The Commissioner may allow or require the specification to be amended or a new one substituted before the patent issues.

**Official Examination.**—A more or less complete official examination is made.

**Taxes.**—The patent is subject to the payment of a tax of £2 10s. 0d. before the end of the third year, and of a further tax of £2 10s. 0d. before the end of the seventh year, from the date of the patent.

**Conditions of Grant; working invention.**—The invention should be worked in South Australia within three years from the date of the patent.

**Importing and Marking patented articles.**—The law does not prohibit the importation by the patentee of articles manufactured in accordance with the patent, and does not require patented articles to be marked as such.

There are certain penalties for the unauthorised user of the words " Patent," " By the Queen's Patent," &c.

**Revocation of Patent.**—Every patent is liable to be revoked upon the application of a third person after the expiration of three years from the date of granting the patent, if it shall be made to appear to the Governor that neither the patentee nor his assignee or licensee has used the patented invention to a reasonable extent for the public benefit. The Governor has absolute discretion as to refusing such application. Patents may also be revoked or cancelled by writ of *scire facias.*

**Amendments and Disclaimers.**—Errors or defects in the specification or title may be subsequently amended, and disclaimers may be entered, not being such alterations or disclaimers as would have the effect of extending the scope of the grant. If the patent be partly assigned, the assignee must join in the application to amend or disclaim.

**Assignments.**—Assignments must be registered within six months of their date, and must be certified as correct for the purposes of the Act. Every assignment shall be deemed null and void as against any subsequent assignment for valuable consideration, unless such prior assignment shall be registered before the registration of the subsequent assignment. Assignments may be in any suitable form, and as ordinarily prepared for Great Britain will answer every purpose.

# Western Australia

——o——

7his was originally known as the Swan River Settlement. The population in 1881 was 30,200. Lead, copper, zinc and iron exist in considerable quantities. The chief town is Perth.

*(Act No. 1 of 36th Victoria.)*

Letters Patent and Letters of Registration are granted. The former, however, can only be obtained for inventions not already patented elsewhere, while the latter, which have the same force as Letters Patent, are issued when Letters Patent have been granted in other countries. The following abstract therefore includes only those provisions of the law which relate to Letters of Registration.

**To whom Granted.**—Letters of Registration are granted to any person being the holder or assignee of any patent granted or issued and in full force in Great Britain or any other country including bodies corporate and companies as well as individuals.

**Duration of Privilege.**—The Letters of Registration remain in force during the continuance of the original patent in the country in which it was issued or granted.

**Extent of Grant.**—The privilege extends to the colony of Western Australia.

**Official Examination.**—A formal examination of the documents only is made.

**Taxes**—The grant is not subject to any taxes after issue.

**Conditions of Grant; working invention.**—The patentee is under no obligation to put his invention into practice.

**Importing patented articles.**—The importation of patented articles into the colony, by the patentee, is not prohibited.

**Revocation of Grant.**—The grant may be repealed by writ of *scire facias* for the same causes and in the same manner as any grants of the Crown are liable to be repealed.

**Amendments and Disclaimers.**—Errors or defects in the specification or title may be subsequently amended, and disclaimers may be entered, not being such alterations or disclaimers as will have the effect of extending the scope of the grant.

**Assignments, &c.**—Assignments, &c., must be recorded in the office of the Colonial Secretary within three months from the execution thereof. Assignments may be in any suitable form, and as ordinarily prepared for Great Britain will answer every purpose.

# New Zealand.

———o———

This is a British colony in the South Pacific Ocean and comprises three Islands
known as the Northern, Middle and Stewart Islands.    The estimated population
in 1881 was about 481,000.    The resin of the tree—the Kauri pine—known as
Kauri gum, is a valuable export.    Flax is largely exported, but wool is the main
product ; gold, iron, coal, & copper, are found.    The capital is Wellington.

---

### (*The Patents Act,* 1883.)

Letters Patent and Letters of Registration (which have the
same force as Letters Patent) are granted.

By a new law entitled as above, which comes into force on the
1st January, 1884, foreign inventors can at their own option
obtain either Letters Patent, or Letters of Registration, the
restriction by which they were heretofore confined to Letters of
Registration having been removed.    The following particulars
are subject to correction, a copy of the new Act not having been
received at the time of going to press.

**To whom granted.**—Letters Patent can only be granted
to the inventor, not to his assignee.    Letters of Registration
are granted to the inventor or to the holder or assignee of
Letters Patent or any like protection issued in Great Britain, or
any other colony, and which are in full force.

**For what granted.**—Letters Patent are granted for any
manner of new manufactures within New Zealand.    Letters of
Registration are granted for the subject matter of any Letters
Patent or like privilege issued in Great Britain or any other
colony, and which are in full force.

**Novelty of Invention.**—In order to obtain valid Letters
Patent the invention must be new, but the validity of Letters of

Registration is not affected by the publication of the invention prior to the application therefor.

**Duration of Patent.**—The duration of Letters Patent is 14 years, subject to the payment of a tax (see *Taxes*), and to the condition as regards working the invention (see *Conditions of Grant*). Letters of Registration remain in force only during the continuance of the previous original foreign patent, and are not subject to the payment of any subsequent tax, but are probably subject to the same condition as Letters Patent as regards working the invention.

**Date of Patent.**—Letters Patent are dated as of the day of application.

**Extent of Grant.**—The privilege, whether granted by Letters Patent or Letters of Registration, extends to the colony of New Zealand, and its dependencies.

**Procedure.**—Letters Patent are obtained by filing a specification and drawings (if necessary) in duplicate. The application may be opposed, but when not opposed will be granted as a matter of course. Letters of Registration will be granted as a matter of course on proof of the *bonâ fide* ownership of the foreign patent, but the procedure for obtaining Letters of Registration is not settled at the time of going to press.

**Official Examination.**—A formal examination of the documents is made.

**Taxes.**—Letters Patent are subject to the payment of a tax of £7 before the expiration of five years from the date of the patent. Letters Patent are not subject to the payment of any tax after application.

**Conditions of Grant; working invention.**—Inventions protected by Letters Patent must be brought into practical operation in New Zealand within two years from the date of the patent, otherwise the patent will lapse. It is not clear whether the same requirement applies in the case of inventions protected by Letters of Registration, but it is probable that the grant is subject to the same condition in this case also.

**Importation of patented articles.**—The importation of patentedarticles by the patentee into the colony is not prohibited. There are certain penalties for the unauthorized user of the words " Patent," " Letters Patent," &c.

**Revocation of Patent.**—The grant may be repealed by writ of *scire jucias.*

**Assignments and Licenses.**—Assignments and licenses must be recorded in the Register of Proprietors, and until the proper entry has been made the grantee of the Letters of Registration is deemed to be the sole and exclusive - proprietor thereof. Assignments may be in any suitable form, and as ordinarily prepared for Great Britain will answer every purpose. Before any assignment or license executed out of New Zealand can be registered, the assignee or licensee must furnish (1) a statutory declaration, by one of the attesting witnesses to the said assignment or license, of the due execution of the said assignment or license. Provided that if it be proved to the satisfaction of the Patent Officer that the attesting witness to any such assignment or license is dead or cannot be found, the execution of the said assignment or license may be proved by a statutory declaration of any other person capable of declaring the same. (2) A certified copy or copies of the assignment or license, and other instruments or documents of title. (3) A statutory declaration by the applicant that he is the person named in the copy deed, and that it is a true copy of the original deed.

The terms used in these regulations are to be interpreted as follows, viz.: (1) A statutory declaration means a declaration made in Great Britain, or Ireland, or any British colony, or New Zealand, before a justice of the peace, notary public, or any other person having authority to take or receive a declaration, under any law for the time being in force; and if made in any foreign country, means a like declaration made before a British consul or vice-consul, or other person having authority to take or receive such a declaration under any Act of the Imperial Parliament for the time being in force, authorizing the taking or receiving thereof. (2) A certified copy means a copy of any deed or instrument, certified by a statutory declaration as aforesaid or by a notary public to be a true and correct copy, and shall include any such copy under the seal of any patent office or other department issuing such patent, and certified under the hand of any commissioner or other officer, of such office or department, to be a true copy thereof.

No assignment or license of two or more Letters of Registration included in one deed or instrument will be registered.

# Tasmania.

——o——

This is an island in the South Pacific Ocean, formerly known as Van Diemen's Land. The population in 1881 was estimated to be 116,000. Wool is the staple product. Tin and iron ore are largely produced; gold is also found, and coal in many parts. The Capital is Hobart Town.

*(The Patent Law Act, 1858.)*

The Governor, with the advice of the Executive Council, is empowered in the name and on behalf of the Queen to issue Letters Patent for any manner of new manufactures within the colony.

**To whom granted.**—Patents are granted to the true and first inventor within the colony.

**For what granted.**—Patents are granted for the sole working or making of any manner of new manufacture within the colony.

**Novelty of Invention.**—The invention is considered new if it has not been published or made known in Tasmania.

**Duration of Patent.**—The duration of the patent is fourteen years from the date of the patent, subject to the payment of the taxes hereafter mentioned (see *Taxes*) and to the limitation (in the case of foreign inventions) to the duration of the prior foreign patent which shall first expire. If the foreign patent has already expired prior to the grant of the colonial patent, the latter is invalid. Provision is also made for the extension of a patent in certain cases beyond the term first granted, the application for extension being referred to Commissioners appointed to enquire into the matter.

**Date of Patent.**—The patent dates from the day of filing the application.

**Extent of Grant.**—The patent extends to the colony of Tasmania.

**Procedure.**—A petition to the Governor, accompanied by a complete specification and drawings (if necessary), is lodged at the office of the Colonial Secretary, and thereupon protection conferring all the rights of Letters Patent is granted for six months.

The application is completed by giving notice to proceed, at which stage the application is advertised in the official gazette and colonial newspapers, and opportunity afforded for the entry of oppositions. The Law Officer may call in such scientific or other aid, as he may deem fit, and cause proper remuneration to be paid therefor, and after considering the application, and hearing any objections, he may issue his warrant for the Letters Patent, which are thereupon prepared and are sealed by the Governor with the seal of the colony. The Law Officer may allow or require the specification to be amended, or a new one substituted, before the patent issues.

**Official Examination.**—A formal examination is made.

**Taxes.**—The patent is subject to a tax of £15 payable prior to the expiration of the third year, and to a further tax of £20 prior to the expiration of the seventh year, from the date of the patent. The Letters Patent must be returned in order that these payments may be endorsed thereon.

**Conditions of Grant; working invention.**—The law imposes no obligation on the patentee to put the invention into practice in the colony.

**Importation and Marking of patented articles.**—The importation by the patentee of the patented articles is not prohibited, and the patentee is under no obligation to mark the patented articles in any way. There are certain penalties for the unauthorized user of the word " Patent," " By the Queen's Patent," &c.

**Revocation of Patent.**—Letters Patent may be repealed by writ of *scire facias* in like cases as the same would lie in England for the repeal of Letters Patent.

**Amendments and Disclaimers.**—Errors or defects in the specification and title may be subsequently amended, and disclaimers may be entered, not being such alterations or disclaimers as would have the effect of extending the scope of the grant.

**Assignments and Licenses.**—All assignments and licenses must be recorded, and in the absence of the proper entry the grantee is deemed the exclusive proprietor of the patent· Assignments may be in any suitable form, and as ordinarily prepared for Great Britain will answer every purpose.

# British Guiana.

———o———

The chief product of British Guiana is sugar, which is the finest in the world and known as Demerara crystals. Coffee, cocoa, and rum are also produced. The colony is divided into three counties—Berbice, Demerara, and Essequibo, and comprises an area of about 85,000 square miles. The administration of the colony is in the hands of a Governor and Court of Policy, consisting of four official and five non official members. The capital is Georgetown. The population of the colony in 1881 was about 252,000.

*(The Patent Law Ordinance, 1861).*

The Lieutenant-Governor is empowered to grant in the name of Her Majesty, and under the public seal of the colony, patents for the sole privilege of making, using, exercising, and vending any new manufacture in the colony.

**To whom granted.**—Patents are granted to the true and first inventor within the colony.

**For what granted.**—Patents are granted for any manner of new manufacture within the Statute of Monopolies (21 James I., cap. 3.)

**Novelty of Invention.**—The invention must not have been publicly used or exercised in the colony prior to the application for patent therein.

**Duration of Patent.**—The duration of the patent is fourteen years from the date of the patent subject, however, to the payment of a tax (see *Taxes*). In the case of an invention first invented in the United Kingdom or elsewhere, and for which a patent has there been obtained prior to the grant of a patent in the colony, the duration of the colonial patent is dependent on the continuance of the previous foreign patent, or if several, its duration is limited by that of the one which shall first expire. A valid patent in the colony cannot be obtained after the expiration of a patent for the same invention in the United Kingdom or any other country.

**Date of Patent.**—The patent is usually antedated as of the day of application, but it may be dated as of any day between that date and the actual day of sealing.

**Extent of Grant.**—The patent extends to the whole colony of British Guiana, which comprises the counties of Demerara, Essequibo, and Berbice.

**Procedure.**—A petition and affidavit accompanied by a provisional or a complete specification, are lodged and referred to the Attorney-General, who may call in scientific assistance. Upon his allowance provisional or complete protection is acquired for 12 months, during which time the invention may be used and published. Complete protection confers moreover the same rights as Letters Patent during that period. Notice to proceed must be given within three months from the date of the Attorney General's report, whereupon the application is advertised for one month, during which period objections may be lodged. The Attorney General reports to the Governor upon the application and upon any objection thereto, which report is advertised. In case of an adverse report an appeal lies to the Supreme Court. If favorable, the Governor then directs the Letters Patent to issue. The Letters Patent must then be registered in the Registrar's Office for the counties of Demerara, and Essequibo, within ten days from the date of sealing, and lastly a complete specification must be filed within six months from the date of the patent if a provisional specification was lodged in the first instance.

**Official Examination.**—The application is referred for examination to the Attorney General, who may call in scientific aid, if necessary, and may require amendments to be made.

**Taxes.**—The duration of the patent is subject to the payment of a tax of 100 dollars before the expiration of the 7th year from the date of the patent, the amount of which tax must be stamped on the patent.

**Conditions of Grant ; working invention.**—The law imposes no obligation on the patentee to put the invention into practice in the colony.

**Importation and Marking of patented articles.**— The law does not prohibit the importation by the patentee of articles manufactured in accordance with the patent, and does not require the patented articles to be marked as such.

**Amendments and Disclaimers.**—Disclaimers of any portion of the invention, and alterations of the specification may be made, the procedure being similar to that on an original application.

**Prolongation and Confirmation of Patent.**—The Governor is empowered to prolong the term for which the patent was originally granted, for a period not exceeding seven years, and to confirm invalid patents in certain cases.

**Assignments and Licenses.**—Assignments and licenses, whether complete or partial, must be registered in the colony.

# British Honduras.

———o———

This is a British colony in Central America. The portion of the soil capable of cultivation is very fertile, but the only important cultivated products are sugar and tropical fruits. Coffee of excellent quality can also be grown, but little attention has hitherto been devoted to this. The colony comprises about 6,500 square miles. The capital is Belize, with a population in 1881 of 5,767.

---

(*The Patent Law Amendment Act*, 1862.)

Letters Patent are granted for any invention, being any manner of new manufacture the subject of Letters Patent and grant of privilege within the meaning of the Statute of Monopolies.

The Governor and the members of the Executive Council (together with other persons who may be appointed by the Governor) are Commissioners of Patents, and the powers vested in the Commissioners may be exercised by any three or more of them. Three or more of the Commissioners are empowered to subscribe their names to warrants for Letters Patent under the Act.

**To whom granted.**—Patents are granted to the true and first inventor within the colony of British Honduras.

**For what granted.**—Patents are granted for any manner of new manufacture, the subject of Letters Patent and grant of privilege within the meaning of the Statute of Monopolies (21 James I., cap. 3). No Letters Patent will, however, be granted for two or more distinct substantive inventions contained in a single application.

**Novelty of Invention.**—The invention must be new within the colony.

**Duration of Patent.**—The duration of the patent is fourteen years from the date of the application, subject, however, to the payment of the taxes hereafter mentioned (see *Taxes*), and to the condition, in the case of an invention for which a previous foreign patent has been obtained, that all rights and privileges shall cease and be void immediately upon the expiration or other determination of the term during which the foreign patent shall continue in force, or, in the case of more than one foreign patent, on the determination of the term which shall first expire (see also *Prolongation*).

**Date of Patent.**—The patent is usually antedated as of the day of application.

**Extent of Grant.**—The patent extends to the whole colony of British Honduras.

**Procedure.**—A petition and declaration, accompanied either by a provisional specification (or a complete specification, particularly describing and ascertaining the nature of the invention, under the hand and seal of the applicant), is lodged at the office of the Colonial Secretary, and referred to the Attorney General for the colony. The Attorney General, if a provisional specification be lodged, has power to call in scientific or other aid, and order due remuneration to be paid therefor. If satisfied that the invention is properly described, the Attorney General issues a certificate of allowance of Provisional Protection for six months. Notice to proceed is then given, and the application is advertised in such manner as the Commissioners may deem fit, and opportunity for the entry of oppositions afforded. The case is then again referred to the Attorney General, together with any objections that may have been lodged. A warrant for sealing is then made, granting to the applicant, his executors, administrators, and assigns, the sole right of making, using, exercising, and vending the invention for the term of fourteen years.

**Official Examination.**—No examination is made as to the novelty or utility of the invention.

**Taxes.**—The patent is subject to the payment of a tax of 50 dollars before the expiration of three years from the date of the patent, and a further tax of 100 dollars before the expiration of seven years from the date of the patent, which payments must be endorsed on the patent.

**Conditions of Grant; working invention.**—The law imposes no obligation on the patentee to put the invention into practice in the colony.

**Importation and Marking of patented articles.**— The law does not prohibit the importation by the patentee of articles manufactured in accordance with the patent, and does not require patented articles to be marked in any way.

**Amendments and Disclaimers.**—Disclaimers of any portion of the invention and alterations of the specification, not being such disclaimers or alterations as would extend the right obtained, may be made.

**Prolongation of Patent.**—The Commissioners are empowered to grant new Letters Patent for a further term of not more than fourteen years after the expiration of the first term.

**Assignments and Licenses.**—All assignments, &c., must be recorded in the " Register of Proprietors " at the Colonial Secretary's office, and until this is done the grantee is deemed the exclusive proprietor of the patent.

# British India.

———o———

British India extends over a territory as large as Europe without Russia, and is divided into the three Presidencies of Bengal, Bombay and Madras.

Native manufactures have been in parts almost superseded by the importation of products from Europe, and especially from the United Kingdom. In certain districts they are however still extensive, and the annual value of cotton, woollen and silk goods from manufactories in the Punjaub, is estimated at about £5,000,000. In Bombay Presidency the manufactories of cotton goods has made considerable progress. There are also considerable silk manufactures in the Bombay Presidency, and also in Bengal and the central provinces, and jute in Bengal. The annual value of exports from India is now estimated at £59,000,000. The principal exports are opium, raw cotton, seeds, rice, jute, hides and skins, tea, indigo, and wheat. The population at the last census was about 241,000,000.

Accounts are kept in rupees (=about 2s.) annas (=1½d.) and pice (=⅛ of a penny.) Considerable sums are reckoned by lacs and crores (i.e. 100,000, and 10,000,000) of rupees.

———————————————

Exclusive priviliges for making, selling, and using inventions in India of any new and useful manufacture are granted by the Governor General in Council, to the inventor.

**To whom granted.**—Exclusive privileges are granted to the actual inventor (whether native or foreign) or his personal representatives, and also to the assignee of the actual inventor of the right to obtain the privilege in India. The mere importer of an invention into India is not deemed an inventor unless he be the assignee of the actual inventor.

**For what granted.**—Exclusive privileges are granted for any new and useful improvement in any art, or process, or manner of producing, preparing or making an article and also any new and useful article produced by manufacture.

**Novelty of Invention.**—In the case of an invention for which an English patent has already been obtained, the application for an exclusive privilege in India must be made within twelve months from the date of the English Patent, and the invention is deemed new if it has not been publicly known or used in India before the date of the English Patent, notwithstanding that it may have been publicly known or used in England or in India after that date, and before filing the application for the exclusive privilege in India.

In other cases the invention must not have been used by the public, or made known by a printed or written publication in the United Kingdom or in India before the filing of the application, but the use of the invention in public by the inventor, his deputies &c., for one year prior to the filing of the application, is not deemed a publication.

**Duration of Privilege.**—The duration of the exclusive privilege is fourteen years, but contingent on the continuance of the previous English Patent (if any) for the same invention. The term may be extended if the English Patent be prolonged.

**Date of Privilege.**—The date from which the duration of the exclusive privilege runs, is the date of filing a specification under the Act. This is usually some weeks after lodging the application.

**Extent of Grant.**—The patent extends to the whole Empire of India, but not to the native States.

**Procedure.**—A petition to the Governor General of India in Council, for leave to file a specification, is first presented in due form, and may be referred to an expert for inquiry and report. An order is then made to file a specification, to which order such conditions and restrictions may be annexed as the Governor General may think fit. The specification must be filed within six months of the date of such order, and thereupon the exclusive privilege is acquired.

**Official Examination.**—No examination is made as to the novelty or utility of the invention, a formal supervision only of the documents being exercised.

**Taxes.**—The duration of the exclusive privilege is not subject to the payment of any taxes after the first application.

**Conditions of Grant; working invention.**—The law imposes no obligation on the patentee to put the invention into practice in India.

**Importation and Marking of patented articles.**—The importation into India by the patentee, of articles forming the subject of the exclusive privilege is not prohibited, and there is no obligation to mark the patented articles in any way.

**Revocation of Privilege.**—The exclusive privilege ceases if the Governor General in Council shall declare the same, or the mode in which it is exercised, to be mischievous to the State or prejudicial to the public. Moreover upon breach of any special condition annexed to the order to file the specification being proved, the Governor General may declare that the exclusive privilege shall cease. Any person may also apply to the Supreme Courts to declare the exclusive privilege not to have been acquired in consequence of non-fulfilment of the requirements of the law. If an exclusive privilege be obtained in fraud of the actual inventor, the Courts may, on proof thereof and on proceedings instituted within two years, order the privilege to be assigned to the actual inventor and the profits to be paid to him.

**Amendments and Disclaimers.**—Errors or defects in the specification may be subsequently amended, and disclaimers may be entered to any part of the invention which should not have been included.

**Assignments and Licenses.**—All assignments &c., must be duly entered and recorded in the Patent Office, Home Department, Government Offices, Calcutta.

# Cape of Good Hope.

———o———

This is a British Colony at the south extremity of Africa. The population in 1875 was about 721,000. The principal agricultural products are wheat, oats, maize, millet, and barley. Rice and tobacco are also grown in certain parts. Some excellent wine is made, notably Constantia. The most important industry is sheep rearing, and the export of wool averages nearly two thirds of the total exports. Mohair is also exported, and Ostrich farming has recently developed considerably. The capital is Cape Town.

---

### (*Act No.* 17, *of* 1860.)

The Governor is empowered to grant Letters Patent for the sole and exclusive working, making, and enjoyment of any invention within the colony for the term of fourteen years.

**To whom granted.**—Patents are granted to the true and first inventor within the colony. In the absence of any judicial decision on the subject in the colonial Courts, the Judges would undoubtedly follow the English precedents, and therefore the expression true and first inventor within the colony may be construed to include the importer as well as the actual inventor.

**For what granted.**—Patents are granted for any invention being any manner of new manufacture within the meaning of the Statute of Monopolies (21 James I., cap 3).

**Novelty of Invention.**—The invention must not have been published or publicly used or exercised within the colony prior to the application for the patent.

**Duration of Patent.**—The duration of the patent is fourteen years from its date, subject however to the payment of taxes before the expiration of the 3rd and 7th years respectively and the endorsement of such payments on the Letters Patent (see *Taxes*).

The duration of the Cape patent is limited to that of the shortest patent obtained elsewhere for the same invention, prior to the grant of the colonial patent. A Cape of Good Hope patent granted for an invention for which a patent elsewhere has already expired is of no validity.

**Date of Patent.**—The Letters Patent are dated as of the day of deposit of the specification.

**Extent of Grant.**—The patent extends to the whole colony of the Cape of Good Hope, including the Diamond Fields.

**Procedure.**—Complete protection is granted for six months from the date of deposit of the specification, which confers the rights of Letters Patent and permits of the invention being used and published without prejudice to the patent. Notice to proceed must then be given within such time as will enable the inventor to take out the patent before the expiration of protection, and an appointment advertised in the Government Gazette and other colonial papers. The application is then referred to the Attorney General to hear any objections to the grant. The Attorney General may call in scientific assistance and order costs to be paid. The Attorney General may then issue a warrant for Letters Patent, subject to any restrictions, etc., he may think fit. The Letters Patent may issue to the executors of inventor deceased during protection, and they may be repealed or withheld, and the specification cancelled.

**Official Examination.**—No examination is made as to the novelty and utility of the invention but the application is referred for examination to the Attorney General who may require the title or the specification to be amended, or a new one substituted.

**Taxes.**—The duration of the patent is subject to the payment of a tax of £10 before the expiration of the third year, and £20 before the expiration of the seventh year, from the date of the patent, and such payments are to be endorsed upon the patent.

**Conditions of Grant ; working invention.**—The law imposes no obligation on the patentee to put his invention into practice in the colony.

**Importation and Marking of patented articles.**— The importation of the patented articles from abroad by the patentee is not prohibited, and the law does not require them to be marked " Patent."

**Revocation of Patent.**—The patent may be repealed by a writ of the Supreme Court in the nature of a writ of *scire facias* in England. The patent is void if the invention be contrary to law, or generally prejudicial or inconvenient, or if the invention was not new within the colony, or if the patentee was not the true and first inventor within the colony, or if the specification is insufficient. The patent lapses by neglect to pay the taxes within the prescribed time (see *Taxes*).

**Amendments and Disclaimers.** — Disclaimers and alterations of the specification may be made, the proceedings being similar to those on an original application.

**Prolongation and Confirmation of Patent.**—The Governor is empowered to prolong the term of the patent, and to confirm invalid patents.

**Assignments and Licenses.**—The assignment of any Letters Patent, or of any share or interest therein, or any license under Letters Patent, must be registered in the colony. Until so registered the original grantee is deemed sole proprietor of the patent.

# Canada.

The Dominion of Canada comprises the provinces of Ontario, Quebec, New Brunswick, Nova Scotia, Prince Edward Island, Manitoba, District of Keewatin, North West Territories, and British Columbia.

The population is about 4,362,000. A decimal system of coinage has been introduced into the Dominion, according to which the unit of account is a dollar of 100 cents. The average rate of exchange makes the dollar equal to about 4/-. A new and uniform system of weights and measures has also been lately introduced, making the Canadian standards the same as the British Imperial standards, but the British cwt. of 112 lbs. and ton of 2240 lbs. are superseded by the United States equivalents of 100 lbs. and 2000 lbs. respectively.

Iron is found in great quantity in the province of Ontario, and copper, lead, plumbago, antimony, arsenic, manganese, gypsum, and even gold, are found, besides marble and building stone. Large quantities of petroleum and salt are also obtained.

Iron of superior quality is found almost everywhere in the province of Quebec, and gold, copper, lead, silver, zinc, and platinum are also found. Shipbuilding is extensively carried on at the town of Quebec, but the manufactures are comparatively unimportant.

In New Brunswick, and also in Nova Scotia, shipbuilding is also extensive; coal and iron ore are found in large quantities; the deposits of antimony in New Brunswick are exceedingly valuable, and manganese, copper, lead, silver, and gold are also found in both provinces. In British Columbia gold, coal, iron, copper, bismuth, mica, and limestone are found.

---

*(The Patent Act of* 1872, *and Amending Acts of* 1882 *and* 1883.)*

The Act constitutes a Patent Office and appoints a Commissioner of Patents, by whom patents are granted for the Dominion of Canada, which embraces not only the provinces of Ontario and Quebec, but also Nova Scotia, New Brunswick, Prince Edward Island, Manitoba and British Columbia.

**To whom granted.**—Patents are granted to the actual inventor, or to his assignee, or to both inventor and assignee conjointly, or to the representative of a deceased inventor.

**For what granted.**—Patents are granted for any invention of, or improvement in, any new and useful art, machine, manufacture, or composition of matter, not known or used by others before being so invented. But not for any invention having an illicit object in view, nor for any mere scientific principle or theorem. Two or more separate inventions connot be claimed in one patent.

**Novelty of Invention.**—The invention must not have been patented in any foreign country for more than one year, nor may it have been in public use or on sale in Canada with the inventor's consent or allowance, for more than one year prior to filing the application for Canadian patent. The invention may therefore have been published and used in other countries, and it may have been in use and on sale in Canada, for not more than one year, without destroying the validity of the Canadian patent; but if any person commences to manufacture the invention in Canada before the foreign inventor applies for his patent such person will have the right to continue manufacturing and selling the article, notwithstanding the existence of the patent. It is therefore unwise to delay applying for the Canadian patent.

**Duration of Patent.**—The term for which the patent is now granted is 15 years, subject to the payment of the taxes hereafter mentioned (see *Taxes*), and to the limitation that the Canadian patent shall expire at the earliest date at which any foreign patent for the same invention expires, whether such foreign patent be previous or subsequent to the Canadian patent. Canadian patents heretofore issued for shorter terms than 15 years, and in respect of which the fee required for the whole or any unexpired portion of the term of 15 years has been duly paid, shall be deemed to have been issued for the full term of 15 years subject to the same conditions as to payment of taxes as in the case of patents now issued for such full term.

**Date of Patent.**—The duration of the patent is computed from a few days after the date of filing the application.

**Extent of Grant.**—The patent extends to the provinces of Ontario and Quebec, Nova Scotia, New Brunswick, Prince Edward's Island, Manitoba, and British Columbia.

**Procedure.**—The application is made by filing an oath, petition and duplicate specification and drawings. A model or specimen is also required, but this need not accompany the application, as the patent will be granted and have full force without it, but will not be issued before the model is supplied. The applicant must elect his domicile in Canada. The Commissioner may refuse the application in whole or in part upon the grounds that the invention is not patentable; or that it is already in the possession of the public with the consent and allowance of the inventor; or that it is devoid of novelty; or that it has been described in a book, or other printed publication before the date of application, or is otherwise in possession of the public; or that it has already been patented in Canada (or elsewhere for more than one year), except however when the Commissioner has doubts as to whether the patentee or the applicant is the first inventor. Amendments of claims are usually called for, the application being rarely rejected *in toto.* The application must be perfected within two years after lodging the petition, otherwise it will be deemed abandoned. In case of refusal the applicant may appeal to the Governor in Council. If it is found that two applications are made for similar inventions, the question of priority is settled by arbitration.

**Official Examination.**—An examination as to the novelty and utility of the invention is made before the patent is granted.

**Model.**—A model or specimen must be furnished before the patent will be actually issued, although the patent may be applied for and granted without waiting for a model.

**Taxes.**—The applicant may at his option pay the full fee required for the term of fifteen years, or the partial fee required for the term of five years, or that for ten years, and in case a partial fee only is paid, the amount will be stated on the patent, and the patent will cease at the end of the term for which the partial fee has been paid, unless at or before the expiration of that term, the holder of the patent pays the fee of £4 or £8 for the further term of five years or ten years respectively, and takes out from the Patent Office a certificate of such payment in the prescribed form to be attached to and refer to the patent, and under the signature of the Commissioner, or another member of the Privy Council.

**Conditions of Grant ; working invention.**—The law enacts that the patent shall become void at the end' of two years from its date, unless the patentee or his assignee shall within that period have commenced, and shall afterwards continuously carry on, in Canada the construction or manufacture of the invention or discovery patented, in such manner that any person desiring to use it may obtain it, or cause it to be made for him at a reasonable price at some manufactory or establishment for making or constructing it in Canada. In case of inability to comply with this requirement the time may be extended on good cause shown, and on application made within three months before the expiration of the two years.

The above clause of the law is not interpreted literally to mean that the patentee, on penalty of forfeiture, shall actually fabricate the invention with his own capital and keep stock whether he has purchasers or not, but its real meaning has been held by the Commissioner of Patents (who is the sole judge in the matter) to be, that the patentee must be ready either to furnish the article himself or to license the right of using, on reasonable terms, to any person desiring to use it and expressing such desire by a *bonâ fide* serious and substantial proposal, *i.e.*, the offer of a fair bargain accompanied with payment. As long as the patentee has been in a position to hear and acquiesce in such demand, and has not refused such a fair bargain proposed to him, he has not forfeited his rights. In short the words "to carry on in Canada the construction or manufacture" with their context have been held to mean nothing else than that any Canadian citizen has a right to exact from the patentee a license to use the invention patented, or obtain the article patented, for its use, at the expiration of the two years delay on condition of applying to the owner for it and on payment of a fair royalty. To bring the patentee within the scope of this interpretation, his address should be known so that applications or propositions may be made to him, or that he should appoint an agent for the purpose, or arrange with a Canadian manufacturer to make the invention. The same recommendation may be made as in the case of German patents, namely to advertize the invention and notify the willingness of the patentee to grant licenses or indicate the address where the patented article may be purchased. In this way the patentee will comply with the law to the utmost of his ability, where from the nature of the case it would be impossible to actually put the invention into practical operation in Canada (see also further conditions under *Importation and Marking patented articles*).

**Importation of patented articles.**—The importation of the manufactured article into Canada by the patentee, is allowed for one year from the date of the patent. An extension (not exceeding 12 months) of the term during which importation is permissible, may be obtained on good cause shown and on application made within three months before the expiry of the first year. If after the period of one year (or any extension thereof that may be allowed) the patentee or his assignee imports the invention or causes it to be imported, the patent will be void.

Here again the law is not interpreted literally, but the question whether a patent has become null and void by reason of importation after the expiration of the above named period (or any extension thereof), is to be settled by the Commissioner of Patents, by whom it has been held that whilst the importation in commercial quantities, in defiance of the law, and to the injury of the manufacturing interests of Canada, would entail the invalidity of the patent, yet the importation of a few machines as models, or for the purpose of bringing the usefulness of the invention before the invention before the eyes of the Canadian public, and so creating a demand for it, with the intention of supplying such demand, would not invalidate the patent.

**Marking patented articles.**—Every patented article must be marked with the word " Patented," followed by the year in which the patent was granted, under penalty of a fine of £20. When from the nature of the article it is impossible to mark it, then it must have affixed to it, or to the package containing it, a label so marked.

**Amendments and Disclaimers.**—If by inadvertence the specification be insufficient, or claim too much, the patent may be surrendered by the patentee, his assignee, or legal representative, and reissued on an amended specification. Or a disclaimer may be entered of anything included by mistake.

**Assignments and Licenses.**—Every assignment and license, whether total or partial, must be registered in the office of the Commissioner. The deed must be accompanied by a copy on foolscap, which will be retained, the original being returned with a certificate of registration.

# Ceylon.

———o———

This is an island in the Indian Ocean belonging to Great Britain. Its area is about 24,702 square miles, and the population in 1881 was nearly 3,000,000.

The most important product is coffee. The manufactures do not possess much importance, the articles, chiefly made being handkerchiefs, tablecloths, towels, sail-cloth, &c., of a coarse description. There are many oil mills for expressing the oil from cocoa nut kernels. The exports are principally coffee, tea, cinnamon, cocoa nut oil, and coir.

———

## (*Inventions Ordinance,* 1859.)

The Governor in Council is empowered to grant under the public seal of the island of Ceylon the sole and exclusive privilege of making, selling and using any new invention for the term of fourteen years.

**To whom granted.**—Patents are granted to the actual inventor, or his personal representative or his assignee, or to the first importer of an invention not publicly known or used in Ceylon.

**For what granted.**—Patents are granted for any new and useful art, process, or manner of producing, preparing, or making an article, and also any new and useful article prepared or produced by manufacture.

**Novelty of Invention.**—The invention is deemed new if it has not been publicly used in Ceylon prior to the application for a patent. The public use of an invention prior to the application for a patent is not deemed a public use if the knowledge of the invention has been obtained surreptitiously, or in fraud of the inventor, or in breach of confidence, provided the inventor makes his application within six months after the commence-

M

ment of such public use, and has not previously acquiesced in such public use. The use of the invention in public by the inventor himself or his licensee is not deemed a public use provided the invention has not thereby been dedicated to the public.

**Duration of Patent.**—The duration of the patent is fourteen years. The Governor is empowered to grant a prolongation for a further term not exceeding fourteen years.

**Date of Patent.**—The date from which the duration of the patent is computed is the date of filing a specification of the invention in pursuance of an order of the Governor.

**Extent of Grant.**—The patent extends to the island of Ceylon.

**Procedure.**—A petition for leave to file a specification having been filed and referred for enquiry and report, the Governor may make an order subject to such conditions as he may think expedient, whereupon a specification accompanied by a declaration must be filed within six months from the date of such order.

If an English Patent has been previously obtained for the invention the Governor is empowered, upon petition stating the the date and duration of such patent, to make an order authorizing the petitioner to file a specification of the invention and an exemplification of the English Patent granted to him, whereupon the petitioner is entitled to the exclusive privilege in Ceylon for fourteen years.

**Official Examination.**—No examination is made as to the novelty or utility of the invention.

**Taxes.**—The patent is not subject to the payment of any tax after the first application.

**Conditions of Grant ; working invention.**—The law imposes no obligation on the patentee to put the invention in practice in the island.

**Importation and Marking of patented articles.**—The law does not prohibit the importation from abroad by the patentee, of articles manufactured in accordance with the patent, and does not require patented articles to be marked in any way.

**Revocation of Patent.**—No person shall be entitled to an exclusive privilege in Ceylon if the invention, at the time of presenting the petition, was not new in Ceylon (see *Novelty of Invention*), or if the petitioner is not the inventor or the importer of the invention into Ceylon, or if the specification does not particularly describe the invention and the mode of carrying it out. And any person may apply to the District Court of Colombo to declare that an exclusive privilege has not been acquired on any of the following grounds, (*a*) that at the time of filing the petition, the invention, or any part thereof, was not new (see also *Novelty of Invention*); (*b*) that the petitioner was not the inventor or importer of the invention or any part thereof, and in addition thereto, either that the applicant was the inventor or importer, or that the inventor has dedicated or made known the invention to the public, or has acquiesced in the public use thereof (see also *Novelty of Invention*); (*c*) that the nature of the invention, or any part thereof, or the mode of carrying it out, is insufficiently described and defined in the specification, and that such defect or insufficiency was fraudulent and is injurious to the public; (*d*) that the petitioner has fraudulently inserted in the petition or specification, as part of his invention, something which was not new (see *Novelty of Invention*), or whereof he was not the inventor; or (*e*) that the petitioner has wilfully made a false statement in his petition.

The Queen's Advocate may apply to the said Court for a rule calling on the petitioner to show cause why the question of the breach of any special condition on which leave to file a specification was granted, or any other question of fact on which the revocation of the exclusive privilege by the Governor may depend, should not be tried in the form of an issue directed by the said Court; and if the rule be made absolute, the Court, unless the breach, or other matter of fact, be admitted, may thereupon direct such issue to be tried, and certify the result of such trial to the Governor. If at the trial it shall appear that by reason of any of the objections mentioned, the exclusive privilege has not been acquired, the Court will give judgment accordingly, and thereupon the petitioner will, as long as the judgment remains in force, cease to be entitled to the exclusive privilege.

If on any such application to the Court to declare the patent void, on the ground of want of novelty, or insufficiency of specification, the Court shall think that something has been included which was not new, or that the specification is defective or insufficient, but that the error, defect, or insufficiency was not fraudulently intended, the Court may adjudge the patent valid, save as to the part so affected, or may adjudge the whole patent to be valid, and order the specification to be amended. Misdescription in the petition, if not fraudulent, will not defeat the exclusive privilege.

If upon proceedings instituted within two years from the date of a petition to file a specification, the inventor proves that the petitioner was not the inventor, and that he knew or believed the invention to have been obtained, directly or indirectly, in fraud of the inventor, or by means of a confidential communication made by the actual inventor, the Court may compel the petitioner to assign to the inventor any exclusive privilege obtained, and to account for, and pay over, the profits thereof.

An appeal lies from all decisions and orders of the District Court of Colombo to the Supreme Court, and from the latter to Her Majesty in Council.

# Fiji Islands.

—o—

These are a group of Islands in the South Pacific Ocean belonging to Great Britain. The chief are Viti Levu, (Great Fiji) and Vanua Leva, (Great Land). The soil is very fertile, and the principal products are cocoanut, sugarcane, banana, plantain, and cotton. The total population in 1880 was 13,198. The capital is Suva in Viti Levu.

### (*The Patent Ordinance*, 1879.)

The Governor in Council is empowered to grant in the name of the Queen, and under the seal of the colony, Letters Patent for the sole and exclusive privilege of using, selling, or making new and useful inventions in the colony, for the term of fourteen years subject to the conditions hereafter mentioned.

**To whom granted.**—Patents are granted to the true and first inventor within the colony, his heirs, executors, administrators, and assigns. The expression true and first inventor within the colony would, if the decisions of the English Courts be accepted as precedents, include the mere importer as well as the actual inventor, and this is probably the case, but in the absence of judicial decisions in the colonial courts nothing positive can be affirmed on this point. In the case of inventions already patented in England, the holder of the English Patent is entitled to a patent in the colony.

**For what granted.**—Patents are granted for any manner of new manufacture, and also every new process of manufacture, and every new method of application of known processes, and improvements in any known process. The patent may not include several distinct and separate inventions, but where one invention is applicable to several manufactures, or several inventions are applicable to one and the same manufacture, the whole may be included in the same Letters Patent. A valid patent cannot be obtained for an invention, the subject of an English or foreign patent which has already expired.

**Novelty of Invention.**—The invention must be new within the colony at the time of presenting the petition.

**Duration of Patent.**—The duration of the patent is fourteen years, subject, in the case of inventions previously patented in England or elsewhere out of the colony, to the condition that the colonial patent shall expire with such previous English or foreign patent or with the first of them if more than one. If the English or other patent has expired before the application for the colonial patent, the latter is invalid.

**Date of Patent.**—The duration of the patent runs from the date of the Letters Patent.

**Extent of Grant.**—The patent extends to the colony of Fiji and its dependencies.

**Procedure.**—The application is made by filing a petition and declaration accompanied by a complete specification and drawings (all in duplicate) at the office of the Colonial Secretary, and is referred to the Attorney General, who if he deems the invention *primâ facie* entitled to protection issues his Certificate to that effect, whereupon protection conferring all the rights of Letters Patent is acquired for six months. In case of refusal an appeal lies from the decision of the Attorney General to the Governor in Council, a month being allowed for this purpose. Notice to proceed is to be given and advertised twice in the Royal Gazette and one other colonial paper within two months from the date of the protection, and any oppositions to the grant of Letters Patent must be entered within three months from such advertisement. If none be entered, the Attorney General is to report accordingly to the Governor in Council, or in case of opposition he is to hear the parties and their witnesses and report his decision to the Governor in Council, who, if there be no opposition, or if the decision be favorable, will direct the issue of Letters Patent within three months from the date of such report. In case of an adverse decision an appeal lies to the Governor in Council.

**Official Examination.**—No examination is made as to the novelty or utility of the invention.

**Taxes.**—The patent is not subject to the payment of any taxes after the first application.

**Conditions of Grant; working invention, &c.**—The law imposes no conditions as to working the invention in the colony, nor as to importing or marking the patented articles.

**Revocation.**—The Attorney-General may apply to the Supreme Court to cancel or revoke the patent on the ground that the invention is of no utility, or was not new at the date of application; or that the applicant is not the true and first inventor thereof; or that the petition or specification contains a wilfully false statement. The Supreme Court may order the specification or petition to be amended.

Letters Patent may be annulled by the Governor in Council if the same be proved prejudicial, or if the special conditions on which the same were granted are not observed.

**Amendments.**—A specification may be amended on application to the Attorney-General, from whose decision an appeal lies to the Governor in Council.

**Assignments.**—Assignments and Licenses must be registered in the office of the Registrar-General in the colony.

# Gibraltar.

———o———

This is a town and strongly fortified rock in Spain, at the entrance of the Mediterranean, belonging to Great Britain. The area of the possession is about two square miles, and the population in 1878 without the garrison was upwards of 18,000.

————————————

There is no Patent Law for this dependency, but special ordinances are obtainable, granting the exclusive privilege of making, selling, and using inventions which have been patented in Great Britain. The only ordinances as yet granted have related to inventions for improvements in, and connected with, electric telegraphs.

**To whom granted.**—Exclusive privileges are granted to the grantee of the Letters Patent in the United Kingdom, their executors, administrators, and assigns.

**For what granted.**—Exclusive privileges are granted for the invention comprised in the English Patent or Patents.

**Duration of Privilege.**—The duration of the exclusive privilege is limited to the unexpired residue of the term of the English Patent, including any prolongation thereof.

**Procedure.**—His Excellency the Governor of Gibraltar may, upon petition filed, enact an ordinance granting the exclusive privilege, subject to approval and confirmation by Her Majesty, and to the filing, within six months of such approval, in the registry of the Supreme Court, of a certified copy of the English Letters Patent and specifications.

**Disclaimers.**—Disclaimers entered in respect of the English Patent may, upon similar proceedings, be extended to Gibraltar.

# Hong-Kong.

———o———

This is a British possession of some importance off the south east coast of China at the mouth of the Canton river. In 1881 the imports from Great Britain alone amounted to upwards of £3,800,000, and the exports to Great Britain to £1,016,000, the chief export being tea. The population in 1876 was upwards of 139,000.

*(Patent Law of July 3rd, 1862.)*

The Governor in Council is empowered to grant patents for inventions which have already been patented in England.

**To whom granted.**—Patents are granted to the inventor or to the owner, by assignment or otherwise, of the exclusive right to the invention within the colony.

**For what granted.**—Patents are granted for any invention already patented in England.

**Novelty of invention.**—The invention must not have been publicly used within the colony before the date of application.

**Duration of Patent.**—The duration of the colonial Patent is limited to that of the English Patent, or to any less term, at the discretion of the Governor. If the English Patent be prolonged, the colonial patent may be extended also, or a new one granted for a like period.

**Procedure.**—A petition in due form to the Governor is made by the English patentee, his agent, assignee, or personal representative, accompanied by a declaration and specification, identical, as far as possible, with the specification filed on the petition for Letters Patent for the said invention in England. Letters Patent granted under this ordinance confer all the rights and privileges of, and subject the patentee to all the provisions affecting, Letters Patent in England, as fully as if the latter were extended to this colony.

**Conditions of Grant; working invention, &c.—** The law imposes no conditions as to working the invention in the colony, nor as to importing or marking patented articles.

# Jamaica.

——o——

This is the largest of the British West Indian Islands.  It has an area of 4256 square miles and a population in 1881 of 580,804.

The principal agricultural products are sugar, coffee and pimento ; after these maize, tobacco, ginger and arrowroot.  The chief exports are sugar, rum, and tobacco.

Kingston is the capital and seat of government.

———————

*(The Patent Law Amendment Act,* 1857).

The Governor is empowered to grant in the name of Her Majesty, and under the seal of the Island of Jamaica, Letters Patent for the exclusive privilege of making, constructing, using and vending any new invention, discovery, or improvement, for the term of 14 years, and to grant Certificates of Addition for improvements on the subject of the original patent  (see *Certificates of Addition*).

**To whom granted.**—Patents are granted to the true and first inventor within the island, and his personal representatives, and to the assignee of any person who may have taken out Letters Patent for his invention in any other country ; but in the case of an invention made abroad for which no foreign patent has been obtained, the assignee cannot obtain the colonial patent.  The expression true and first inventor within the colony, would, if the decisions of the English Courts be recognized as precedents, include the mere importer as well as the actual inventor, and this is probably the case ; but in the absence of judicial decisions in the colonial courts nothing positive can be affirmed on this point. It is to be noted in this connection that the colonial Act expressly provides that in case of doubt as to the construction of the Act, it may be construed by analogy to the laws in force in England, so far as the same may be applicable.

**For what granted.**—Patents are granted for any new and useful art, machine, manufacture, or composition of matter not theretofore known in the Island, or for any improvement in any such invention and discovery. A valid patent cannot be obtained for an invention the subject of a foreign patent which has already expired.

**Novelty of Invention.**—The invention may have already been patented elsewhere, but must not have been introduced into public and common use in the colony prior to the application for the colonial patent.

**Duration of Patent.**—The duration of the patent is fourteen years from its date, with power of prolongation in certain cases for a further term not exceeding seven years. If, however, the invention has been patented elsewhere prior to the application for the Jamaica Patent, the duration of the latter will be limited to that of the previous foreign patent which shall first expire. A valid Jamaica Patent cannot be obtained for the subject of a previously expired foreign patent. In any case the duration of the Jamaica Patent is subject to the condition hereafter mentioned as to working the invention (see *Conditions of Grant*).

**Date of Patent.**—The patent is usually dated as of the day of application, but it may be dated as of any day between that date and the date of actual sealing.

**Extent of Grant.**—The patent extends to the Island of Jamaica.

**Procedure.**—The application is made by a petition containing a short description of the invention, accompanied by a declaration and a complete specification of the invention, in such full clear and exact terms as to distinguish the same from all other things before known or used in the Island, together with drawings (if any), to which may be added a model or a specimen.

The latter may however be, and is usually, dispensed with. If the applicant be the assignee, the assignment duly proved, and an affidavit setting forth the date of the 'foreign patent, must accompany the application. The application is referred to the Attorney-General, who may call in scientific assistance and order costs thereof to be paid. The application having been duly allowed must be advertised together with a general description of the invention in the Official Gazette and one other colonial newspaper, whereupon the Letters Patent may be issued.

**Official Examination.**—There is no official examination as to the novelty or utility of the invention, but the documents are referred to the Attorney-General for approval.

**Taxes.**—The patent is not subject to the payment of any tax after the first application.

**Certificates of Addition.**—Improvements on an invention for which a patent has already been obtained may be protected by a certificate, to be annexed to the original patent, and to expire therewith, the proceedings being similar to those on an original application.

**Conditions of Grant; working invention.**— The invention must be brought into operation in the colony within two years from the date of the patent, otherwise the patent will become void.

**Importation and Marking of patented articles.**— The law does not prohibit the importation by the patentee of articles made under the patent, and does not impose any obligation to mark the articles patented.

**Amendments and Disclaimers.** — Patents void by reason of a defective description, or by reason of claiming too much, may, provided the error has arisen by inadvertence, and without any fraudulent intention, be surrendered and re-issued upon an amended description. Disclaimers and alterations of any part of the specification may also be entered.

**Assignments.**—Assignments and licenses, whether of the whole or any part of the patent, must be registered in the office of the Island Secretary.

**Infringements.**—Patents may be deemed good and valid in law for so much only of the invention as shall be proved to be the patentee's own, and of new invention, provided it be a substantial part of the thing patented; and suits may be maintained in respect of any infringement of such new part, although the specification may embrace more than the patentee has a legal right to claim. Infringers are liable to pay a sum equal to three times the actual damage sustained by the patentee by reason of such infringement, such damages being recoverable by action in the Supreme Court of the Island.

# Mauritius.

———o———

Mauritius, or the Isle of France, is an island in the Indian Ocean. The chief town is Port Louis. There are numerous islands dependent on the Governor of Mauritius, the chief being Rodriguez and the group of the Seychelles. In addition to these there is the group of the Amirante Islands, and several others, producing principally cocoa nut oil. Sugar is the principal product of Mauritius, after which come coffee, cocoa, rice, indigo, and spices. The principal exports in addition to sugar are aloes, fibre, vanilla, cocoa nut oil and rum.

———————————

*(Ordinance No.* 16 *of* 1875.)

Patents of Invention are granted by the Governor for fourteen years for any new invention.

**To whom granted.**—Patents are granted to the actual inventor whether native or foreigner, and his personal representatives, and also to the assignee of the actual inventor. In case of joint inventors, the patent must be in their joint names. The importer into Mauritius of a new invention is not deemed an inventor unless he be the actual inventor.

**For what granted.**—Patents are granted for new and useful discoveries, new or improved chemical products, new or improved modes of applying known processes or forces whereby a new or improved product or preparation is made, and also any new or improved art, process or manner of producing, preparing or making an article, and also any new or improved article prepared or produced by manufacture.

No patent will however be allowed to include several distinct and separate inventions, but where one invention is applicable to several manufactures, or several inventions are applicable to

the same manufacture, the whole may be included. No patent
will be granted for an invention the subject of an expired
foreign patent.

**Novelty of Invention.**—If an English Patent has already
been obtained for the same invention, the holder of the English
Patent must apply in Mauritius within 12 months of the date
thereof, and in that case publication of the invention in
Mauritius between the date of the English Patent and the date
of application in Mauritius is not material. In other cases the
invention must not have been publicly used or published either
in Mauritius or in the United Kingdom of Great Britain and
Ireland, prior to petitioning for the Mauritius Patent. The
user in public by the inventor, his servants, or licensee, for not
more than one year prior to the date of petitioning for the
Mauritius Patent, does not deprive the invention of the attribute
of novelty, nor does public use or publication of the invention
by others for not more than six months, if a knowledge thereof
has been obtained surreptitiously or in fraud of the inventor.

**Duration of Patent.**—Patents are granted for fourteen
years from the date of the patent, and may be prolonged for any
period not exceeding fourteen years in addition, as the Governor
General in Council may deem fit. When an English Patent
for the same invention has already been obtained, the duration
of the Mauritius Patent is dependent on the continuance of the
English Patent. A valid Mauritius Patent cannot be obtained
for an invention, the subject of a foreign patent which has
already expired.

**Date of Patent.**—The date from which the patent runs is
the date of application.

**Extent of Grant.**—The patent extends to the colony of
Mauritius and its dependencies, comprising the Seychelles
Islands, and Rodrigues.

**Procedure.**—A petition accompanied by the necessary
documents is filed in the office of the Colonial Secretary, and
is referred to the Procureur-General, by whom protection for

six months is granted. In case of an adverse decision an appeal lies to the Governor in Council. The application must then be advertised in the Government Gazette within two months of the certificate of protection. Objections to the grant of the patent may be entered within one month from the date of advertisement and may by consent be heard by the Procureur-General; otherwise they are referred to the Supreme Court for decision. Before the patent is sealed a printed copy of the petition and specification must be deposited.

**Official Examination.**—No examination is made as to the novelty or utility of the invention.

**Taxes.**—The patent is not subject to any tax beyond the fees on application.

**Conditions of Grant; working invention.** — The law imposes no obligation to put the invention into practice in the colony.

**Importation and Marking of patented articles.**— The law does not prohibit the importation by the patentee of articles made in accordance with the patent, and there is no necessity to mark the patented articles.

**Revocation.**—The patent may be cancelled if it be proved to the satisfaction of the Governor in Council that it is prejudicial to the public, or that any special condition upon which it was issued has been broken. Any person may also apply to the Supreme Court to declare that the patent shall be revoked, for want of novelty or utility of the invention, for insufficiency of the specification, or because the patentee is not the inventor within the meaning of the law.

**Amendments and Disclaimers.**—Amendments to correct errors, defects, or insufficiencies in the petition or specification, or to disclaim old parts erroneously claimed, may be made by petition, declaration, and memorandum, or specification, in the same way as an original application.

**Assignments and Licenses.** — The assignment of a patent must be registered in the colony.

# Natal.

—o—

This is a British colony on the south-east coast of Africa, having an area of 18,750 square miles and a population of about 400,000. The principal products are sugar, indigo, coffee, arrow-root, tobacco and rice. Sheep's wool is the most important export and after this raw sugar, coffee, hides and skins. The chief mineral productions are coal and lime.

### (*Colonial Act No. 4 of* 1870.)

Patents are granted by the Lieutenant Governor for the sole and exclusive working, making, and enjoyment of any invention for any term not exceeding fourteen years, subject to the conditions and taxes hereafter mentioned.

**To whom granted.**—Patents are granted to the true and first inventor within the colony. In the absence of any judicial decision on the subject in the colonial Courts the judges would undoubtedly follow the English precedents, and therefore the expression, true and first inventor within the colony, may be construed to include the importer as well as the actual inventor.

**For what granted.**—Patents are granted for any manner of new manufacture within the meaning of the English Patent Law. A valid patent cannot be obtained in Natal for an invention the subject of a foreign-patent which has already expired.

**Novelty of Invention.**—The invention must not have been publicly used in Natal before the application for the patent.

**Duration of Patent.**—The duration of the patent is fourteen years from the date of application, but subject to the payment of certain taxes (see *Taxes*), and to the condition that, in case of an invention first invented out of the colony, and for which a patent has been obtained elsewhere before application for the colonial patent, the life of the colonial patent is dependent on that of the prior foreign patent which shall first expire. If a foreign patent for the same invention has lapsed prior to the grant of the colonial patent, the latter has no validity.

**Date of Patent.**—The patent dates and runs from the day of application.

**Extent of Grant.**—The patent extends to the colony of Natal.

**Procedure.**—A provisional specification, signed by the applicant, may be deposited in the first instance, whereby six months' protection is acquired, conferring the same powers, rights, and privileges, as Letters Patent, including the right to use and publish the invention. This provisional specification is kept secret for six months, and the Attorney General may require it to be amended.

In lieu of a provisional specification, a complete specification fully describing the invention may be filed whereby similar privileges are acquired for six months. In either case notice to proceed must be given eight weeks before the expiration of the protection, and an appointment obtained, which must be advertised in certain newspapers at the applicant's expense, whereupon objections may be entered to the grant.

The Attorney General having heard and disposed of such objections (if any) may then issue a warrant for the Letters Patent, subject to such conditions as he may deem proper. Application must be made to seal the patent within three months from the date of the warrant and before the expiration of the protection (except in case of accident). The Letters Patent are then issued in accordance with the terms of the warrant.

**Official Examination.**—No examination is made as to the novelty or utility of the invention, but the application is referred to the Attorney General for perusal.

**Taxes.**—The duration of the patent is subject to the payment of £5 and £10 before the expiration of the 3rd and 7th years respectively from the date of the patent.

**Conditions of Grant; working invention.**—The law imposes no obligation to put the invention into practice in the colony.

**Importation and Marking of patented articles.**—The importation by the patentee of the patented articles is not prohibited, and they are not required to be marked in any way.

**Amendments and Disclaimers.**—The patentee or his assignee may enter disclaimers and amendments to the specification to which opposition may be entered, the procedure being similar to that on an application for patent.

**Prolongation and Confirmation of Patent.**—Power is provided for the extension of the patent for a term not exceeding fourteen years beyond the original term for which it was granted, and for its confirmation in case of invalidity, the proceedings being under the jurisdiction of the Supreme Court.

**Assignments and Licenses.**—Assignments and Licenses whether complete or partial must be registered in the colony before they can have any validity.

# Newfoundland.

——o——

This is an island of British North America, at the mouth of the Gulf of St. Lawrence. having an area of 40,200 square miles, and a population of upwards of 170,000. The capital is St. John's, and this is the only town of any considerable importance in the island. The chief exports are fish, fish and seal oil, seal skins, and copper ore. Labrador is a dependency of Newfoundland.

---

### (*Patent Law of* 1856.)

The Governor is empowered to grant Letters Patent under the Great Seal of the Island, for the term of fourteen years, conferring the full and exclusive right and liberty of making, constructing, using, and vending, new and useful inventions.

Improvements made subsequent to the date of the patent may be incorporated with the original grant (see *Certificates of Addition*).

**To whom granted.**—Patents are granted to the inventor or holder of Letters Patent in some other country, or to his assignee. But in the case of an invention made abroad, for which no foreign patent has been obtained, the assignee cannot obtain the colonial patent.

**For what granted.**—Patents are granted for any new and useful invention, discovery, or improvement in any art, machine, or composition of matter. A simple change in the form or proportions of a machine, or composition, in any degree, is not deemed an invention (see also *Novelty of Invention*).

**Novelty of Invention.**—The invention must not have been known or used, either in the Island or elsewhere, except it has been patented in some other country, in which case it must not have been introduced into public and common use in the colony prior to the application for a patent therein. No patent is granted for an invention made abroad but not patented there, and a patent granted for the subject of a foreign patent, which has already lapsed, is of no validity.

**Duration of Patent.**—The duration is fourteen years from the date of the patent, which term may be extended for a further term of seven years. In the case of an invention previously patented in some other country, the colonial patent lapses with the expiration of the previous foreign patent which may first expire (see also *Conditions of Grant*).

**Extent of Grant.**—The patent extends to the whole colony of Newfoundland.

**Procedure.**—A petition to the Governor, accompanied by an affidavit, and a full and complete specification, clearly describing and distinguishing the invention (together with drawings, if necessary), are to be delivered to the Colonial Secretary, together with a model or specimens of ingredients and composition of matter. The model may, however, be dispensed with. The application having been referred to the Attorney-General to be examined, and duly advertised for four weeks in the Royal Gazette and one other colonial newspaper, the Letters Patent are issued.

**Official Examination.**—No examination is made as to the novelty or utility of the invention, but an examination of the documents is made.

**Certificates of Addition.**—A patentee may, upon like proceedings as in the case of an original application, annex to his original specification, a specification of an improvement upon his origina invention, and thereafter it will have the same effect in law as if it had been embraced in the original specification and recorded therewith.

**Conditions of Grant; working invention.**—The invention must be brought into operation in the colony within two years from the date of the patent, otherwise the patent will become void.

**Importation and Marking of patented articles.—** The law does not prohibit the importation by the patentee of articles manufactured in accordance with the patent, and does not require the patented articles to be marked in any way.

**Amendments and Disclaimers.**—Disclaimers of any portion of the invention may be entered, and the patent may be surrendered and re-issued upon an amended specification.

**Assignments.**—Assignments of patents must be duly recorded in the office of the Colonial Secretary.

**Infringements.**—Infringers are liable to three times the actual damage sustained by the patentee by reason of the infringement, such damages being recoverable in any superior court of the Island. The patent may be adjudged void upon proof that the specification is insufficient or deceptive, or that the invention was not made by the patentee, but had been in use or described in some public work before the supposed discovery by the patentee, or that the patentee had surreptitiously obtained a patent for the invention of some other person.

A patent may be held |valid in respect only of any material part of an invention, provided it be plainly distinguishable from the remainder, notwithstanding that another portion may, by inadvertence, have been improperly claimed; and suits may be maintained in respect of such part as is actually the patentee's invention although the specification embraces more than he has a legal right to claim.

# St. Helena.

——o——

This is a British possession in the Atlantic, having an area of about 46 square miles. It has a fine natural harbour at James Town, and is an important calling place for ships passing between Europe and the east by the Cape route.

---

## (*Ordinance No. 3 of* 1872.)

Letters Patent granted under the Great Seal of the United Kingdom of Great Britain and Ireland may be extended to, and have the same force and effect in, the Island of St. Helena.

**To whom granted.**—The patent right is granted to the English patentee, his executors, administrators, or assigns.

**For what granted.**—The patent right is granted for the invention for which the English Patent was granted.

**Duration of Grant.**—The duration of the patent right is limited to the unexpired residue of the English patent, including any prolongation thereof.

**Procedure.**—Certified copies of the English Letters Patent and specification are to be filed in the Registry of the Supreme Court.

In all cases of doubt and difficulty not provided for by the Ordinance, or by the local laws of the island, the same shall be guided and governed so far as is practicable by the law in force in England.

# Sierra Leone.

————o————

This is a settlement in West Africa belonging to Great Britain, and comprises the peninsula Sierra Leone, Sherboro Island, and the Isle de Los, having an area of 468 square miles, and a population of about 70,000. The exports are ginger, cocoa nuts, indiarubber, gum-copal, hides, and palm-oil. The capital is Freetown.

*(Ordinance of* 1862.)

All laws and statutes which were in force within the realm of England on January 1st, 1862, not being inconsistent with any Royal Charter in force in this colony, or with any Letter or Letters Patent, or order in Council issued in pursuance thereof, or with any Ordinance in force in this colony, or with any rule made in pursuance of any such Ordinance, shall be deemed and taken to be in force in this colony, and shall be applied in the administration of justice so far as local circumstances will permit.

No Act of Parliament that was not in force in England on January 1st, 1862, shall be in force, or applied in the administration of justice in this colony, unless the Act shall contain words which, by legal construction, would extend the Act to this colony, or unless the Act shall be extended to this colony by an Ordinance of the Legislature of this colony.

# Straits Settlements.

——o——

These are British dependencies in the Straits of. Malacca consisting of the islands of Singapore, Dinding or Pancore, and Penang, the district of Malacca and. the Province Wellesley. They are all subject to the Governor at Singapore. The exports comprise sugar, spices, sago, tapioca, hides, tea, coffee, tobacco, gums.

The population is about 350,000.

### (*The Inventions Ordinance,* 1871.)

Letters Patent are granted by the Governor in Council under the public seal of the colony for the term of fourteen years for any new and useful invention.

**To whom granted.**—Patents are granted to the actual inventor or to the importer of an invention not publicly known or used in the colony, and to the assignee or the executor, administrator, or heir of the inventor or owner of the invention.

**For what granted.**—Patents are granted for any new and useful invention, or improvement, in any art, process, or manner of producing, preparing, or making an article, and also any article produced by manufacture.

**Novelty of Invention.**—The invention must not, prior to the application for patent, have been publicly used by any others than the inventor, his agents, or licensees, either in the United Kingdom, in this colony, or in any other British possession. Prior public use by others upon knowledge surreptitiously or fraudulently obtained, will not defeat the patent provided the latter be applied for within six months of the commencement of such use.

**Duration of Patent.**—The duration of the patent is fourteen years, which may be prolonged for a further term not exceeding fourteen years. If the invention has already been patented in the United Kingdom, or in any British possession, the duration of the colonial patent will be limited to the term for which such British or other patent may remain in force.

**Date of Patent.**—The date from which the duration of the patent runs is the date of filing the specification.

**Extent of Grant.**—The patent extends to the whole colony of the Straits Settlements.

**Procedure.**—If the invention has already been patented in the United Kingdom, or in any British possession, the Governor may, on petition stating the date and duration of such patent, authorize the filing of a specification and exemplification of such English or other patent, whereupon the exclusive privilege in the colony will be acquired during the remainder of the term for which such English or other patent may remain in force.

In other cases a petition to the Governor in Council for leave to file a specification, accompanied by a declaration, is first filed, and may be referred by the Governor for inquiry and report. An order authorizing the filing of a specification is then made, subject to such restrictions as the Governor in Council may think expedient. A specification must be filed within six months from the date of such order, whereupon Letters Patent are issued.

**Official Examination.**—No examination is made as to the novelty or utility of the invention.

**Taxes.**—The patent is not subject to the payment of any taxes beyond those on the first application.

**Conditions of Grant.**—The law imposes no obligation on the patentee to bring his invention into practical operation in the colony, does not prohibit the importation by the patentee of articles manufactured in accordance with the patent, and does not require patented articles to be so marked.

**Revocation of Patent.**—The Governor General in Council may revoke the patent if it, or the mode in which it is exercised, be mischievous to the State, or generally prejudicial to the public, or upon proof of breach of any special condition upon which the patent was granted.

Any person may apply to the Supreme Court to declare the patent wholly or partly void, on the ground (*a*) that the invention, or part thereof, was not new at the date of the application for the patent; or (*b*) that the patentee was not the inventor, but that the applicant was the inventor, or that the inventor has dedicated the invention, or part thereof, to the public; or (*c*) that the specification is insufficient; or (*d*) that the patentee has fraudulently included something not new or not of his invention; or (*e*) that the patentee has made a false statement in his petition or specification.

The Court may, in case of want of novelty of part of the invention, or in case of error, defect, or insufficiency, not fraudulently intended, adjudge the patent valid in part; or may adjudge it wholly valid, and order the specification to be amended.

**Amendments and Disclaimers.** — Disclaimers and amendments made to the English or other prior patent may be extended to the colonial patent. In other cases disclaimers may be entered to any part of the invention erroneously claimed as new, or any error, defect, or insufficiency of the specification may be cured or amended.

**Infringements.** — An action for infringement cannot be defended on the ground that the specification is defective, or that the petition or specification contains a misdescription, or that the invention is not useful; nor on the ground that the patentee was not the inventor unless the defendant shows that he is the actual inventor or his assignee. But any such action may be defended on the ground that the invention was not new if the defendant, or some person through whom he claims, proves that he has publicly or actually used the invention or the part infringed, in the colony, or in the United Kingdom, or in any British possession, prior to the application for the· patent.

The patentee of an invention in fraud of the true inventor may, upon the application of the true inventor within two years after the application for the patent, be compelled to assign the patent to the true inventor, and to account to him for the profits thereof.

# Trinidad.

———o———

This island is the next largest of the British West Indies after Jamaica, its area being 1,754 square miles and the population about 154,000. The most important products are sugar, molasses, rum, coffee, and pitch. The capital is Port of Spain.

---

*(Ordinance No. 25, 1867.)*

The Registrar-General of the Island is empowered to issue a Certificate vesting in the applicant his executors, administrators, or assigns the sole right and benefit of using an invention within the island for the term of fourteen years.

**To whom granted.**—The exclusive privilege is granted to the inventor within the colony. This will include the actual inventor, or his assignee, or the importer of an invention into the colony.

**For what granted.**—The exclusive privilege is granted in respect of any new and useful invention.

**Novelty of Invention.**—The invention must not have been publicly used or exercised in the colony prior to the application for the Certificate.

**Duration of Privilege.**—The duration of the exclusive privilege is fourteen years, and is apparently independent of the continued existence of patents for the same invention elsewhere.

**Date of Privilege.**—The privilege dates and runs from the date o the certificate.

**Extent of Grant.**—The privilege extends to the Island of Trinidad.

**Procedure.**—A declaration and specification of the invention are delivered to the Registrar-General, whereupon he will deliver a certificate, which must be advertised in the Royal Gazette. The specification may be delivered open or sealed, and, if sealed, will be opened by the Registrar-General at the expiration of six months, or earlier at the applicant's request, and the specification will thereupon be registered.

**Official Examination.**—No examination is made, either as to the novelty or the utility of the invention.

**Taxes.**—The exclusive privilege is not subject to the payment of any taxes after the fees on application.

**Conditions of Grant.**—The law imposes no obligation to put the invention into practice in the colony, does not prohibit the importation by the patentee of articles made in accordance with the patent, and does not require them to be marked.

**Revocation of Grant.**—The grant will cease, and become void, if it be proved that the invention had previously been publicly used, or exercised in the colony, or that the invention is prejudicial or generally inconvenient.

**Amendments and Disclaimers.**—Disclaimers and amendments may be entered by the grantee or assignee of the certificate of exclusive privilege.

**Assignments.**—Assignments must be duly recorded in the colony.

**Infringements.**—The patentee is entitled to the like remedies against infringers as the patentee of an invention would be entitled to in like case by the law of England.

# The Leeward Islands.

——o——

The Leeward Islands belonging to Great Britain are Antigua, Montserrat, St. Christopher, (or St Kitt's), Nevis, Dominica and the Virgin Islands. By an Act passed in 1871 these colonies were formed into one. The Colony contains about 118,000 inhabitants. Antigua is the most important of the group. The principal productions are sugar, rum, molasses, coffee and lime juice.

---

### (*The Patent Law Act*, 1876.)

Letters Patent are granted for the exclusive right to make, use, exercise, and vend, new and useful inventions in the Leeward Islands for the term of fourteen years.

**To whom granted.**—Patents are granted to the true and first inventor within the colony. The expression true and first inventor would probably be interpreted as in England, and would in that case include the importer of a new invention into the colony as well as the actual inventor.

**For what granted.**—Patents are granted for any manner of new manufacture the subject of Letters Patent and grant of privilege within the meaning of the existing law of England governing the subject; but not for the subject of an expired foreign patent.

**Novelty of Invention.**—The Invention must not have been known or used in the colony prior to the date of application.

**Duration of Patent.**—The duration of the patent is fourteen years, subject to the payment of the taxes hereafter mentioned (see *Taxes*), and to the condition (in the case of an invention first invented abroad, or by the subject of any foreign power or state, and which has been patented abroad before the grant of the colonial patent) that the colonial patent shall expire with the prior foreign patent which shall first expire. If the foreign patent for the same invention has expired before the grant of the colonial patent, the latter is invalid.

**Date of Patent.**—The patent is dated as of the day of application.

**Extent of Grant.**—The patent extends to the whole of the Leeward Islands comprised by the Colony.

**Procedure.**—The application is made by a petition and declaration accompanied by a provisional or complete specification, and is referred to the Attorney General who may call in scientific assistance if necessary, and order a remuneration to be paid therefor. The Attorney General may thereupon allow the application, whereupon protection is acquired for six months, and the invention may be used and published during that time; and if a complete specification has been filed the same rights are acquired as though Letters Patent had been granted. The application must then be proceeded with and advertised, at which stage objections to the grant may be made by other persons. The application, together with any objections, is again referred to the Attorney General, who after considering the same may order a warrant for the sealing of the Letters Patent which are then sealed by the Governor with the great seal of the Colony. If a provisional specification was lodged in the first instance, a complete specification must be filed within six months from the date of the application.

**Official Examination.**—No official examination is made as to the novelty or utility of the invention.

**Taxes.**—The patent is subject to the payment of a tax of £10 before the end of the third year, and a further tax of £20 before the end of the seventh year, from the date of the patent.

**Conditions of Grant.**—The law imposes no obligation to work the invention in the colony, does not prohibit the im-

o

portation of the patented articles by the patentee, and does not require the patented articles to be so marked.

**Amendments and Disclaimers.**—The law provides for the entry of disclaimers of parts of the invention erroneously claimed, and for making amendments to the specification.

**Assignments and Licenses.**—Assignments and Licenses must be registered in the colony, and until so registered the original grantee of the Letters Patent is deemed to be the exclusive proprietor thereof.

# The Windward Islands.

———o———

The British Colonies of the Windward Islands comprise Barbados, St. Lucia, Grenada, St. Vincent and Tobago. The population of the group is about 290,000. The most important product is sugar, and in addition to this Barbados produces rum and petroleum; St. Lucia cacao; Grenada cacao, coffee, spices, &c.; St. Vincent arrowroot and cotton; and Tobago, rum, molasses and coffee. Barbados is the most important of the group.

# Barbados.

———o———

This island has an area of about 106,470 acres. The population is about 172,000.

There is no general legislation relating to patents, but special Acts are passed by the Colonial Legislature, granting to the inventor, his executors, administrators, and assigns, the exclusive privilege of making, using, and vending, new and useful inventions in the island for a term generally of seven years (but sometimes of fourteen years) subject only to the proviso that a specification be filed in the Colonial Secretary's office within three months after the passing of the Act.

o 2

# St. Lucia.

———o———

This island comprises an area of 250 square miles. The population is about 39,000.

There is no general Patent Law in this colony, but a special ordinance is obtainable upon petition to the Governor in Council, conferring the exclusive right to make, use, exercise, and vend, any new and useful invention within the colony for fourteen years from the date of proclamation of the ordinance. Exclusive privileges are granted to the inventor, his executors, administrators, and assigns. The invention must be new as to the public use and exercise thereof within the colony. A specification fully describing the invention must be filed within six months from the date of proclamation of the ordinance. The ordinance usually fixes a penalty of £250 for infringement.

# St. Vincent.

———o———

This island has an area of 132 square miles. The population is about 41,000.

There is no general Patent Law in force in this island, but a special Act is obtainable on petition, conferring on the inventor, his executors, administrators, and assigns, the exclusive right to make, use, exercise, and vend, any new and useful invention in the island for the term of fourteen years, the only condition being the filing of a specification of the invention within six months of the passing of the Act.

# Grenada.

—o—

This island contains about 76,538 acres, and has a population of 43,000.

Letters Patent for inventions not known within the Island of Grenada are granted by the Governor and Legislative Assembly, securing to inventors the exclusive right and privilege of in any way whatsoever using, employing, applying, and vending their inventions within the Island and dependencies thereof for the term of fourteen years.

Proceedings may be taken in a Court of Equity, or in a Court of Law, for protecting the patentee's interests, and for the recovery of damages. The mode of procedure in any suit in an action, and all pleadings with respect thereto, are in conformity with the practice in like cases in the Chancery Division of the High Court of Justice in England.

FINIS.

# INDEX.

Cordingley & Sharpe, Printers, Hammersmith.